NEWGRANGE

Geraldine Stout
and
Matthew Stout

CORK UNIVERSITY PRESS

Published by
Cork University Press,
Youngline Industrial Estate
Pouladuff Road
Togher
Cork,
Ireland

British Library Cataloguing in Publication Data
A CIP catalogue record for this book is available from the British Library.

Paperback ISBN 978-185918-431-8
Hardback ISBN 978-185918-441-7

Printed by Graphicas Cems, Navarra, Spain

This publication has received support from the Heritage Council under the 2008 Publications Grant Scheme.

CONTENTS

PREFACE

Newgrange is the most visited archaeological site in Ireland. Every year 250,000 people come to see this Neolithic passage tomb set in the rich pastureland of County Meath. The visitor is attracted to Newgrange because it is simply the best example of a passage tomb in Western Europe and its solstice phenomenon, in particular, has made it famous throughout the world. It is also conveniently located only an hour from Dublin. When the new millennium was dawning, RTÉ (the Irish national broadcasting company) set the celebrations in motion by broadcasting the winter solstice sunrise at Newgrange to millions of people around the world. While it is the best-known ancient site in Ireland, many aspects of Newgrange are not clearly understood and other aspects are just taken for granted. As two archaeologists with lifetimes of experience in the Boyne Valley, we share with most visitors the same uncertainties about the tomb: why is there a three-metre high quartz wall around its entrance, how does the roof box work, what was the inspiration for its art and architecture? We had given many tours of the Boyne Valley, including Newgrange, but never entirely came to grips with the mysteries of its most prominent monument. We chose to write this book in order to learn more about Newgrange for our own benefit and pleasure, and to present our findings to the general reader. This is our personal interpretation of an intricate and often hotly debated story.

The book is arranged in such a way as to replicate a visit to the site. For those who have been to Newgrange, it will be a reminder of the things that were seen on the tour. It pauses over points of art and construction that the visitor will not have had time to examine in detail on a conventional excursion. *Newgrange* is the synthesis of years of excavation and research at home and abroad, from the detailed reports stemming from the excavations of M.J. O'Kelly – the most advanced for their time – to current international debate about its construction and reconstruction. This is the first book on Newgrange to draw on O'Kellys' private papers and to incorporate the results of more recent and as yet unpublished excavations. This book will clarify many complex issues that have been addressed in widely scattered fora, using original illustrations to assist the reader. It also places the monument in its broader cultural context. Our search for the origins of Newgrange took us to Brittany, Spain, Portugal, Malta, the Orkney Islands and Wales and it has enriched our understanding of its place in European prehistory. This book will enhance the reader's appreciation of the strong links between Newgrange and monuments in the rest of Europe. For those who have not yet been to Newgrange, this book provides a detailed introduction to the history of the site and enhances a later visit. We hope you enjoy reading it as much as we enjoyed writing it.

ACKNOWLEDGEMENTS

This book could not have been written without the assistance of many people. We would like to thank the O'Kelly family for allowing the public to view the O'Kelly papers, and Ann Lynch in the Department of Environment, Heritage and Local Government who administers the collection. Ann Lynch also allowed us access to her excavation results in advance of publication. Clare Tuffy and her staff at Brú na Bóinne Visitor Centre have always provided us with a base from which we can study Newgrange and a place where our theories about the tomb can be bounced off the guides. Thanks also to Con Brogan, Anthony Roche and Patricia Keenan of the Photographic Section in the Department of the Environment, Heritage and Local Government for their continuing encouragement and for providing so many beautiful images. Paul Woods took additional photographs. Thanks to the National Museum of Ireland, particularly Valerie Dowling, Mary Cahill and Griffin Murray, for access to the Newgrange artefacts and photographic images. Peter Moloney photographed many of the finds. Palle Eriksen of the Ringkøbing-Skjern Museum, Denmark and Anthony Pace, Superintendent of Cultural Heritage, Malta have helped us to understand the complexities of Newgrange in an international context. We have consulted widely in the course of producing this book and the degree to which our colleagues have been eager to help is a delightful aspect of working in Irish archaeology. Elizabeth Shee-Twohig provided many publications on megalithic art and John O'Neill rushed photocopies of some more obscure articles to us. Frank Prendergast helped us with the archaeo-astronomy of the solstice phenomenon. Kevin Whelan was the first to observe the important connection between the Knowth phallus and K22, and Finbar McCormick contributed his thoughts on stone balls. Graham Soffe and Richard Abdy helped us assess the relative value of Roman coins. Billy Colfer introduced us to the concept of transporting stones under water and produced the drawing to illustrate the theory. David Dickson first suggested that we write a book on Newgrange for the general public. Thanks to those who read early drafts of this book and made many worthwhile contributions, especially Kevin Whelan and Eileen O'Carroll, the staff at Cork University Press for their encouragement and efficiency. In our tour of the megalithic art of Europe, we are most grateful to Loretto Lacey for providing accommodation in Spain, to Mary Shine Thompson for arranging accommodation in Brittany and Caroline Wickham-Jones for accommodation and access to her library on the Orkneys. We thank all our colleagues in the National Monuments Service and in St Patrick's College, Drumcondra for their support. Finally we thank our girls Nóra and Helen for indulging us in our pursuits.

Geraldine and Matthew Stout
Plougharnel, Brittany and
Julianstown, County Meath, 2008

For Frank, Myrtis, Pearse and Anne, our parents

'*I don't see any reason why I shouldn't take on this dig.
I feel that it will probably be very dull ...*'

M.J. O'Kelly to P.J. Hartnett, 1961

CHAPTER ONE

THE WALL

The first glimpse the eager visitor gets of Newgrange comes when the bus they have taken from the visitor centre reaches the top of McDonnell's lane and, turning west along the road at the crest of the ridge, the passage tomb can at last be seen. It is difficult for two seasoned academics to recall their first impressions of Newgrange from over three decades ago, but for us, as for most first arrivals, it was the starkness of the white quartz wall that registered initially (fig. 1). This wall is three metres high and almost vertical. Its prominence eclipses the decorated kerbstones that lie beneath it and encircle the base of the cairn so that, with the additional height of the kerbstones, the wall rises to a height of over four metres. It contrasts sharply with the grassed over mound that the wall was built to contain. Seamus Heaney, visiting in the dead of winter, observed the 'unsunned tonsure of the burial mound', comparing the modern appearance of Newgrange to the bald heads of Irish monks in medieval times.

If contemporary visitors find that this provides the passage tomb with a startling modern appearance, they are correct. The wall was constructed between 1967 and 1974 following two decades of archaeological investigations. This restoration project was the brainchild of a committee established by the Irish Tourist Board in 1961, which selected Cork archaeologist, Professor M.J. O'Kelly, to lead it. This 1961 Committee had envisioned a different outcome to the wall we see today. The principal aim of the committee was to make the passage accessible to the growing number of tourists and to expose the decorated kerbstones along the circumference of the mound. These had been obscured by the vast bulk of cairn material that had slipped down from the mound and across the kerb in the five millennia after Newgrange was first built. Had their original vision been achieved, the cairn material would have simply been taken from the base of the mound and returned to the top of the cairn. The mound would then have conformed to the universal logic of the angle of repose, the angle that all loose materials eventually assume no matter how vertically they are piled up. The angle of repose is 36° above the horizontal, not the near 90° realised by the quartz wall as it stands today.

The reconstructed quartz wall is based on the professional interpretation of excavation results on the part of M.J. O'Kelly. Numerous sections cut through the mound revealed two critical deposits; a layer of quartz in front of the kerb, and layers of turves behind. The layer of quartz, with interspersed rounded grey granite boulders, was a metre thick nearest to the kerb and it thinned out – as if it had slumped forward – for a distance of seven metres. Behind the kerb there were two thick layers of turves representing up to

CON BROGAN / DoÉH&LG

Fig. 1 Since its construction in the early 1970s, the glaring quartz wall dominates our first impressions of Newgrange.

fourteen individual layers of turf which would have been well over a metre thick when originally laid across the cairn. Subsequently the turf was compressed by the weight of overlying material.

The archaeologist believed that there had to have been a high revetment wall rising from the top of the kerbstones to hold back material because the mound was so much higher than the kerb (fig. 2). The key factor determining the height of this wall was the estimation of the original thickness of the cairn. O'Kelly concluded that the mound was significantly higher than today because the layers of turves would have been appreciably thicker. Having postulated the existence of a retaining wall, he then proposed that the quartz layer represented the remnants of this wall. He describes in his book on Newgrange how he experimented with this startling hypothesis. The quartz from a cutting was built up in a vertical wall over a kerbstone and then forced to collapse. The results were 'well-nigh identical' to the lower layers of quartz and granite uncovered during the archaeological excavations.

A couple of difficulties arise at this point. First of all, no records, photographs or plans of the wall experiments survive in the O'Kelly archive. Secondly, if the wall was original and it behaved as stated, its height of three metres above the kerb remains highly suspect. That height is based on the compressed turf layers in only one section, the deposits behind Kerbstone 95 (the third kerbstone to the right of the entrance stone K1). The section behind K2 (the stone immediately to the right of the entrance stone), shows much thinner turf deposits. To the east of the mound, behind K81, there is only a single thin layer of turves. The evidence does not support the

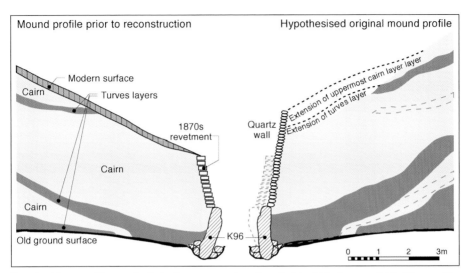

Fig. 2   The profile on the left shows a section face behind Kerbstone K96. The profile on the right shows the original thickness of the turf layers prior to being compressed by the weight of the cairn. The hypothesised height of these layers led Professor O'Kelly to insist on constructing the façade to a height of three metres above the kerb.

construction of so high a wall over such a large section of Newgrange's south-eastern façade.

In the years following the construction of the quartz wall, there have been alternative interpretations of the archaeological evidence. Some believe that the quartz layer was laid out as a terrace in front of the kerbstones. These terraces are a familiar feature of passage tombs on the continent with good examples at Barnenez in northern Brittany (fig. 45) and Alcalar, near Alvor in the Algarve (fig. 52). These terraces look quite like the stone gabions we see today along new roadside facings and as defences against coastal erosion in Ireland. However, the excavations discovered no quartz deposits beneath the kerbstones that had fallen forward at an early stage of the mound's collapse, so it is unlikely that the quartz was piled up in front of the kerb. Further, the shadow-casting phenomena created by the Bronze Age erectors of the Great Stone Circle (more of which in chapter eight) could not have taken place if the kerbstones near the tomb entrance were not still visible. Others suggest that it represented the gradual accumulation of material resulting from ritual activity. The quartz was thickest at the entrance to the passage tomb and the amount of quartz then gradually thinned out, being 'hardly present' twenty kerbstones west of the entrance and sixteen kerbstones east of the entrance, an asymmetry repeated throughout the structure. In support of this argument, they refer to the layers of quartz that were found at the entrances to the passage tombs at nearby Knowth.

Another interpretation challenges the very notion that a quartz wall ever existed at Newgrange. A Danish archaeologist believes that the passage tomb at Newgrange was constructed in a series of distinct phases. The mound was

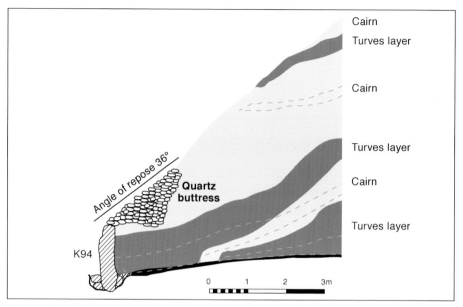

Fig. 3   The probable appearance of the original mound. There is strong evidence for a quartz structure of some type above the kerb but only a low, wide buttress would have had the structural integrity necessary to hold back the passage tomb cairn.

originally much smaller and when the kerb was constructed it was free standing and many metres outside the passage entrance. In this radical interpretation, the mound was a later construction from the Bronze Age in the manner of Silbury Hill in England, completely covering tomb, kerb and quartz. In our opinion the quartz must have stood above the kerb as a low, wide buttress sloping back at the angle of repose, holding back the cairn and turf layers (fig. 3). Placement of reflective stone on the entrance façade of a cairn is a feature of other passage tombs such as Knockroe, County Kilkenny, Loughcrew, County Meath and a tomb at Balnuaran, near Inverness in north-eastern Scotland.

Years ago, we had the privilege of hearing M.J. O'Kelly discuss his work at Newgrange before a large and enthusiastic meeting of the University College Dublin Archaeological Society. We hung on his every word until the end when he showed Newgrange before the excavation and then after its reconstruction. O'Kelly believed that his work breathed 'some faint spark of life into Newgrange', justifying its claims to be 'the mansion of the Good God, the Dagda of early Irish tradition'. He asked 'Which would you prefer?'. Too polite to speak, we said nothing but it must have dawned on everyone there, so soon after the wall was constructed, that it constituted a monumental mistake. This is not to say that Professor O'Kelly was wrong about the monument's original appearance. No one knew Newgrange better than O'Kelly. He took the tomb apart and put it back together again, he literally and figuratively wrestled with the true nature of the passage tomb for a prolonged period between excavation and reconstruction. He had many powerful arguments for the existence of a retaining wall: the quantity of quartz, the thickness of the turves, reconstructions of the wall's collapse, engineers' reports, actual evidence for the wall discovered at the north of the tomb.

Great men, great archaeologists, are rarely troubled by uncertainties. For O'Kelly sufficient evidence existed for the revetment wall on the kerb and he recommended a dry stone wall be built as he believed it would have been constructed in the Neolithic. The architect charged with implementing O'Kelly's vision deemed the construction of so flimsy a structure impractical and unsustainable; after all, the first quartz wall was thought to have collapsed in one sudden event, not a good omen for the safety of future tourists. The cairn is highly unstable and the outward force of the cairn is immense. The erection of a massive reinforced concrete wall rising to a height of four metres from behind the kerbstones along the south-eastern front of Newgrange was the practical solution to implementing O'Kelly's interpretation. The quartz was embedded into the concrete and steel structure and the rounded granite boulders were placed at random, like currants in a quartz scone. The suggestion has been made that the dark granite boulders could have been placed within the wall forming geometrical patterns in the style of the art work on the kerbstones. Happily, this notion was not expressed in the final reconstruction.

The erection of the white quartz wall represented the rejection of the 1961 Committee's view that a 'shapely hemispherical mound of stones' should be reconstructed. In its uniformity, this great wall also fails to mirror excavation results that prove that whatever the angle of original construction, there was a tapering-off on either side of the entrance stone. O'Kelly could not have calculated how long a dry stone wall, built of quartz fragments and rounded granite boulders, would have withstood the pressure of the cairn material behind it. One of the marvels of the construction of the passage tomb within the cairn is that it remained basically intact and almost completely waterproof to this day. It was, in other words, built not for a generation but for all time. Are we to believe that Neolithic engineers, who so ingeniously built the enduring tomb, also constructed so ephemeral a façade?

The quartz wall inflicted a 1960s' standard of office-block design upon a structure that had stood for five thousand years and had been a ruin for four thousand of them. It was the last time in Ireland that scientific opinion, no matter how well founded, and a modern aesthetic would be allowed to impinge so forcefully on the ancient. If it were done again, the current approach to the presentation of ancient monuments would have seen Newgrange restored as unobtrusively as possible; accessible yes, but a ruin. The views of the excavator would be captured in models of the passage tomb to be viewed in the visitors' centre. This was in fact proposed as late as 1971 when there was growing unease with the restoration programme. O'Kelly insisted that his wall be built. As an approach to interpretive reconstruction, new Newgrange is itself a monument to past standards. It stands at the end of a tradition of an intrusive style of presenting ancient monuments throughout the world, reaching from Richard Evans' rebuilding of Knossos in the nineteenth century to Saddam Hussein's assertions in Babylon at the end of the twentieth. It has been included in an international list of the world's worst archaeological reconstructions.

Putting to one side the debate about the wall, the huge quantity of quartz and granite at Newgrange is powerful testimony to the complex belief systems of the Neolithic people who originally gathered this stone together. The truly remarkable feature of these stones is that they were not locally available (fig. 4). The quartz, which contains distinctive white mica flecks, is found only in the Wicklow Mountains away to the south. During the Ice Age there was no movement of ice from south to north, so quartz could not have been transported naturally to the Boyne Valley. The granite boulders have their origins in the Mourne Mountains but the glacier swept these along and gave them their distinctive rounded shape before depositing them in the Cooley peninsula to the north. Different coloured rocks have been used by tomb-builders to enhance the external appearance of passage tombs elsewhere in Ireland, Scotland and Brittany. At Newgrange the effect is strikingly black and white, the quartz embellished with the granite and possibly arranged in geometric patterns, relying mainly on the play of light and shade for visual effect.

How this huge quantity of stone came to Newgrange is a matter of much speculation and one's view is coloured by one's attitude to the wall itself. If the wall originally stood as reconstructed then it is an integral part of the mound's engineering and all the stone had to be available during the construction phase. Accordingly, countless loads of quartz from the south and granite from the north would have been collected and loaded onto boats made of hazel and willow rods, covered with cattle hide. These boats would have then travelled along the coast and up the Boyne; a journey of seventy kilometres for the boatloads of quartz, forty kilometres for the granite. If, however, the quartz and granite at Newgrange were not structural, it could have accumulated over a long period of time. Prehistoric pilgrims to the tomb, probably at the winter solstice ceremonies, might have brought with them a rock from home in the manner of pilgrims in historic times. Naturally, these Neolithic visitors would have longed to place their stone near the entrance, but failing that as close to it as possible. This would explain the tapering off of quartz and granite deposits either side of the entrance. On the other hand, everything seems so well planned, so deliberate when it comes to the construction of this tomb that an impromptu expression of wider devotion is surprising. Whatever the final form of the quartz and granite construction, the shiny white quartz and the prominent position of the tomb would have made it visible from miles around; a spectacular site and the ultimate achievement of this Neolithic civilisation.

The visitor today approaches Newgrange from the south-west and climbing up the gravel path reaches the top of the ridge before turning east to

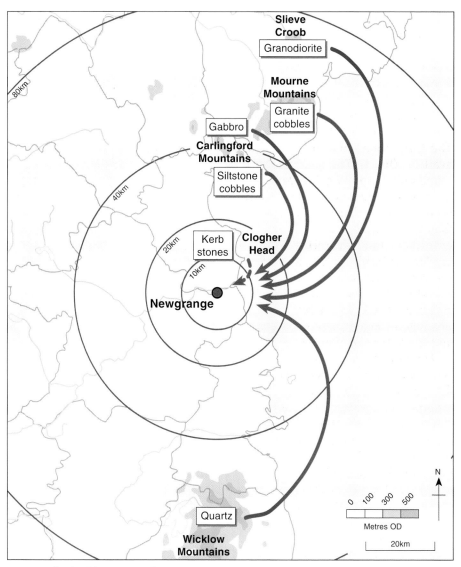

Fig. 4 The building stone for Newgrange was drawn from upland and coastal areas up to eighty kilometres away from the site.

the tomb's entrance. We can never know what sacred rites occurred here but evidence from the Bronze and Iron Ages suggest that ceremonial sites were approached via indirect routes, making the arrival at the object of devotion a sudden and stunning revelation. Our modern route to the passage at Newgrange might indeed emulate this Neolithic procession as it joins with the tomb near its blunted eastern face. The quartz and granite wall sets in stark relief the massive kerbstones beneath. Now, that which is unquestionably authentic comes to the fore.

CON BROGAN / DofEH&LG

Fig. 5   The kerbstones at Newgrange were raised above or lowered below the old ground surface to keep a horizontal alignment. This photo shows K12, the tomb's largest kerbstone. It weights seven tonnes. The quartz wall rises to an improbable height above.

The tomb is delimited by ninety-seven kerbstones. None are missing and the only human intervention since their original placement has been to re-erect those that had slumped forward due to the massive pressure of the enclosing mound. The stones vary considerably in appearance. Some, like the entrance stone and the other highly decorated slabs, have rounded, mammilated shapes. Others kerbstones are graceless blocks of angular rock. These stones range from 1.7m to 4.5m in length (on average they are 2.79m long, 0.45m wide and 0.94m in height). Regardless of their height, the kerbstones are one metre above the old ground surface creating a horizontal line (fig. 5). If the stones were taller than this, they were set deeper into the ground to retain a uniform height; if shorter, they were raised up on boulders of appropriate size. Each kerbstone is thought to weigh between two and five tonnes (three tonnes on average, the weight of a female Asian elephant). End to end the kerb is 270m long and weighs over 300 tonnes, a quarrying and transportation achievement equivalent to the erection of the vault of a gothic cathedral.

How the kerbstones were transported to Newgrange (not to mention the stones which make up its huge chamber) is one of those questions that immediately spring to the mind of even the most casual visitor. It is an

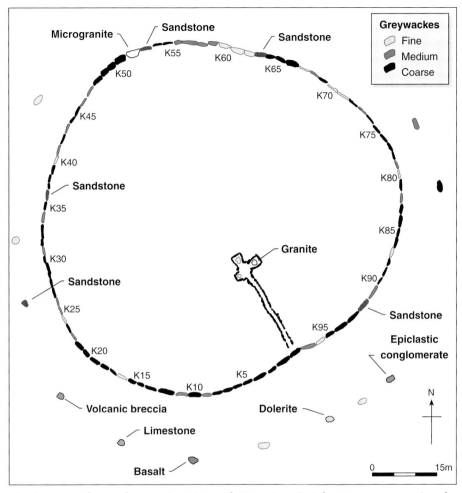

Fig. 6   Research spearheaded by Adrian Phillips identified the stone types used in the construction of Newgrange. They used mostly greywacke quarried from Clogher Head, north of the Boyne Valley. The other stones were glacial erratics which would have been found locally. The great variety of stones used in the Great Stone Circle suggests that it is not contemporary with the passage tomb and it is unlikely to have been constructed from stones left over from the building of the tomb.

achievement no less remarkable for all the many reconstructions we have all seen on television. Neolithic men, perhaps women too, had to find these stones and bring them to the construction site. The traditional view had been that these huge stones were found in the area, deposited by glaciers during the last ice age. But this has been challenged by more concerted geological research. For example, the great passage tomb at Dowth has a kerb of irregular stones, clearly glacial erratics: but none of the stones at Newgrange show any evidence for ice scratch marks that would be expected on stones transported glacially. The construction of Dowth might have exhausted this local supply

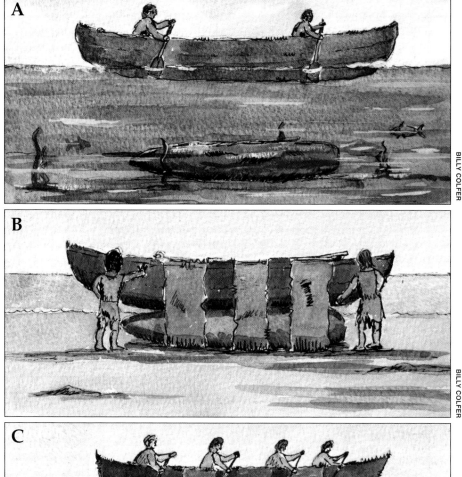

Fig. 7 The kerbstones for Newgrange were quarried at Clogher Head and transported along the coast and up the River Boyne. Strapped beneath a boat, the three tonne stones would have been more portable. A) The megalith is transported to the inter-tidal shore and the boat is positioned over the stone. B) As the tide falls, the boat is positioned on top of the stone. The stone is secured to the boat using cowhides. C) The rising tide lifts the boat and stone, and the crew paddles to Newgrange.

and the more uniform stones at Newgrange had to be gathered from further afield. The kerbstones at Newgrange are all made up of a stone that geologists refer to as greywacke. At the very least this confirms an age-old description of geologists as those who are colour blind, because greywacke is a green-coloured stone. The stones at Newgrange are so uniform as to only reveal their origins to a dedicated quarrying operation. The source of these stones has been identified at Clogher Head, thirty kilometres away, down the Boyne River and a short distance up the coast (fig. 6). This research was still in its infancy when Adrian Phillips sadly passed away. Had he lived, he would have engaged in detailed chemical analysis and a careful study of the riverbeds for dropped stones that would have established beyond doubt the origins of the Newgrange megaliths and proved their route of transportation. The research continues under the direction of George Sevastopulo.

If we accept Clogher Head as the origin of the Newgrange megaliths, their transportation to the tomb remains a source of wonder. A great skin-covered boat may have had the buoyancy to take a stone quarried beside the sea, to have it lashed to the bottom of the boat, and both boat and stone then lifted with the tide (fig. 7). It was in this manner in historical times that, in the south-east of Ireland on the Hook Peninsula in County Wexford, the quarrymen of Herrylock carved out Old Red Sandstone millstones and transported them from cliff edge to harbour. A typical kerbstone weighing three tonnes on dry land would weigh only half that under water – still heavy but much easier to transport. Archaeologists believe that a portion of a huge standing stone was brought to Gavrinis in Brittany in just this fashion (fig. 44). This Breton example provides the only incontrovertible evidence that megaliths were transported by sea for substantial distances. This is known with certainty because this standing stone was decorated before being deliberately broken into three pieces. Two huge portions were transported locally where they were reused as the capstone for the passage tombs known as La Table des Marchands and Er Vinglé near Locmariaquer. But the third portion, on which the carvings complement perfectly the Locmariaquer capstones, was found four kilometres away on the island of Gavrinis, where it too was reused as the capstone of a third passage tomb.

Having been transported thirty kilometres down the coast and up the Boyne, it would then be necessary to drag these great blocks of stone a kilometre in distance and up a sixty metre slope from the bank of the river to the passage tomb site. The movement of the stones was presumably achieved through the use of sleds, or rolled across logs or perhaps across round stones. Megaliths were transported by this latter method on the Mediterranean island of Malta. We are pretty sure that we know how they did it, and certain the task was accomplished – Newgrange is testimony to that – but our understanding should not diminish our sense of wonder that Neolithic communities were able to achieve so much using such simple methods.

The flat-topped cairn enclosed within the kerb is eighty-five metres at its widest point. One is tempted to say diameter and circumference in a

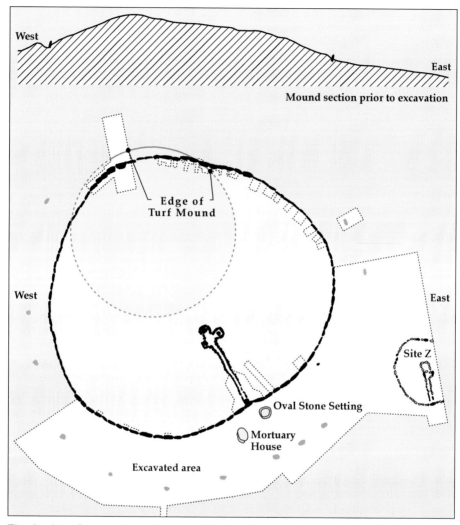

Fig. 8 A turf mound was discovered below the present passage tomb. Its size and function have not been determined but it has yielded a wealth of evidence about the Neolithic environment.

description of its size, but Newgrange is decidedly not circular in plan. For its shape one must imagine a circle with a diameter of eighty-one metres that has been flattened about six metres at its front, facing the southeast, and stretched out about three metres at the back. This produces a flattish and much more imposing entrance where more of the quartz, granite and decorated stones either side of the passage could be appreciated by visitors, both ancient and modern. The passage tomb known as Alcalar 7, near the Algarve holiday resort of Alvor, has a similar flattened façade.

The back of Newgrange might have been elongated to respect and partly enclose the remnants of an earlier tomb. When O'Kelly excavated behind the

Fig. 9   The turf mound of the earlier tomb was 1.5m thick and would have been considerably higher before being compressed beneath the weight of the larger passage tomb cairn.

highly decorated kerbstone (K52), he found evidence for an earlier mound. In excavations undertaken in the 1980s, Ann Lynch also found this turf mound. It may have been thirty-five metres in diameter (figs 8–10). Only the periphery of this mound has been detected; what it covered remains one of the enduring mysteries of Newgrange.

The main mound contained within its ninety-seven kerbstones is massive. It covers half a hectare and is over thirteen metres high. It would have been much higher originally, before the thick layers of turves in the mound were compressed and before tonnes of material spilled out over the defining kerb. The mound is mainly a cairn of loose stones, each larger in size than a fist. There are an estimated two hundred thousand tonnes of these stones. This was a prodigious achievement and one that must have taken years to accomplish. How long it actually took is anybody's guess; variables include the size of an individual load of stones, whether or not draught animals were used, the number of individuals involved, the source of the stone, the length of time each year dedicated to tomb construction, and finally the length of periods when the tomb does not seem to have been under active construction. Twenty or thirty years are the published estimates. It was a project for more than one of the short-lived Neolithic generations. It means that the priest or king who first envisioned the tomb could not see it through to its completion and this individual would have had to impart that vision to at least one younger disciple.

In places, layers of stone are overlain with turves or redeposited sods that gave some stability to the mountain of loose material. These turves were laid

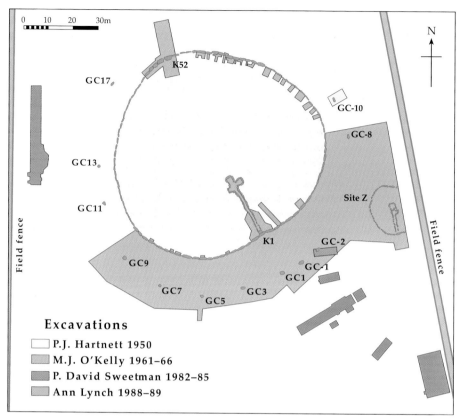

Fig. 10 We know as much as we do about Newgrange due to the large excavated area. There is still much more to be discovered.

in strips from rolled-up turf brought to the mound in the same manner as turf is transported and re-laid by landscape gardeners today. These layers of turf were allowed to become compressed during the construction of the tomb. The excavation in the back of the mound revealed three layers of earth that were most emphatically not redeposited turves. These layers developed naturally on the mound during periods when the cairn material stood exposed to the elements long enough for a layer of sod to develop naturally. It has been argued that these were more than merely prolonged breaks in the construction of the tomb and represent distinct phases in the history of the site. Structural features, such as parallel settings of stones, were used by the builders of the tomb to retain the mound during construction. Settings have been uncovered on other Irish passage tombs and further afield in Iberian tombs such as El Guadalperal, in the Spanish province of Caceres, midway between Lisbon and Madrid.

The excavations showed that the turf was stripped from an area at least one hundred metres distant from the tomb to supply the materials used at Newgrange. One irrefutable conclusion can be drawn from this: the construction of these tombs was important enough to their builders that they were willing to compromise the fertility of large areas of the surrounding farmland. This is a remarkable step for a society to take whose prosperity was founded on the productivity of the land. Thus the passage tomb at Newgrange conceivable represents both the apogee of a civilisation and the origins of its demise.

Today the mound at Newgrange is flat-topped. This is a common feature of the great megalithic tombs of Dowth, Knowth and Newgrange, whereas the smaller tombs have mounds with rounded profiles. The large level area on the top of Newgrange measures forty-five metres in diameter. This is large enough to have functioned as a sacred platform, for ritual fires or the enactment of ceremonies at important times of the year. Two antiquarian reports from the early eighteenth century record a standing stone at the top of Newgrange, emphasising the possibility that the mound top may have been used for ritual activities. A survey of the mound in 1776 shows that this standing stone was removed by that date, but the same survey *does* show a triangular stone located just outside the entrance to the passage. An exact parallel for this arrangement of standing stones – one on top of the mound and one before the entrance – is found at Kercado near the stone alignments in Carnac, Brittany, albeit on a much smaller scale (fig. 50). This alignment outside the tomb meant that astronomical observations could be made from without as well as within the passage. The excavation in front of the tomb did not recover any remains of this triangular stone but there was a 'broad shallow trench' precisely where the stone is depicted in the antiquarian drawing.

Today as visitors are introduced to Newgrange by the guides, their gaze is drawn to the arcadian beauty of the river valley. It is not until one looks out over the valley from the base of the tomb that the true natural wealth and splendour of the setting can be fully appreciated. Newgrange stands above that place on the Boyne that marked the top of the tide in Neolithic times. Where river and sea met the land was especially rich in resources and it was an accessible fording point. A place where the river met the sea may have been seen as a fitting metaphor for a location where the living would commune with the dead. Newgrange is, most importantly, at the focal point of an area known as the Bend of the Boyne, so named because at a point one kilometre to the west of the tomb, the river takes an abrupt turn to the south and swirls around the cairn-topped ridges before again assuming an easterly course near the modern tidal limit at Oldbridge. This is one of the warmest and driest parts of Ireland and its soils are among the richest. It was chosen by the Neolithic farmers for these very reasons, both as land to farm and as a focus for their spiritual world. Forty passage tombs in this small area further emphasise its importance.

Newgrange sits astride a ridge at sixty-one metres above sea level. While the passage tombs of Dowth and Knowth have slightly loftier locations, the verdant richness of the surrounding countryside is best seen from here. In the distance the horizon is described by a continuous 180° sweep of hills. Only at the south-west does a glimpse of the distant, higher hill of Tara (with its own passage tomb), provide a suggestion of the world beyond the Bend of the Boyne and links with the wider Neolithic community of eastern Ireland. There is a distant hint too of the Wicklow Mountains to the south and it is telling that the stones in the quartz façade face their place of origin. In the east the ridge of Dowth is the only place where the horizon is not dominated by the arc of hills on the south side of the river that defines the Bend of the Boyne. Below these hills, again but for the eminence of the Dowth ridge, the full sweep of the river is discernible. Due south and south-west, it can be seen in all seasons, gleaming silver below the clouds or as a starker blue beneath clear skies. In winter and in flood it would not be unreasonable to imagine that Neolithic people made the link between the richness of the valley and their own prosperity.

The ground descends gently from Newgrange in a sequence of broad terraces that form a natural stairway down to the Boyne, and the land everywhere is lush and prosperous. A scattering of smaller, possibly earlier, passage tombs can be seen between Newgrange and the Boyne. These tombs would have reminded the Neolithic pilgrims of their generations-long occupation in the Boyne. As in our own time, it must have been unimaginable to the Neolithic mind that their structures and institutions could be anything other than ageless, that they were in fact mutable and could in time disappear. On occasions of ceremony, a large crowd may have stood before the entrance stone in a gently sloping, almost level area that extends about twenty-five metres in front of the tomb. Beyond this there is a steeper fall to the next terrace. Thousands could have been accommodated on this slope, each with a reasonable view of the activities at the tomb entrance.

Certainly, when the community gathered at Newgrange for the solstice ceremonies in Neolithic times, the view from the mound must have inspired those present to look out across the valley and give thanks for the bounty brought by this earth, before turning to the purpose of the ceremony itself, the celebration of the solstice and commemoration of their dead ancestors. Now at the entrance to the tomb, the modern visitor turns his back to the river and faces a door into the dark, into the intricacies of the passage. The entrance stone at Newgrange becomes our focus and the reason for kerb, cairn and location are finally revealed.

CHAPTER TWO

THE ENTRANCE

Ever since it was built people have known where to enter the tomb at Newgrange. There really is not any need for signs – the builders made it that obvious. Today, the overlying mantle held in by a tight corset of upright stones sucks itself in and the swirling curves on a recumbent stone show the way. The entrance-stone forms a powerful barrier between the living and the dead (fig. 11). It is carved with a triple spiral, each slightly larger than the next, made of a double coil set in anti-clockwise directions. The curving, loose ends of the spirals carry around the foot of the stone in tubular waves and engulf three lozenges, which fill the left edge of the design. The waves break into angular shapes that enclose two lozenges on the right-hand side of the design. A deep vertical groove running halfway down through the centre of the stone divides the upper half of the decoration in two; that on the right is more free-flowing and bolder than that on the left. This deep vertical groove becomes a pair of spirals set in a clockwise direction. Wave-like grooves turn

CON BROGAN / DofEH&LG

Fig. 11 The magnificent entrance stone forms a powerful barrier between the living and the dead.

outwards onto the upper edge of the stone. Decoration straddles its upper rounded contours. The triple spiral is uniquely indigenous to the megalithic art of Newgrange and it is aptly used today in Ireland as a symbol for quality Irish goods. There is one fault: the master carvers had carefully planned out the overall design before the entrance stone was put in place but they did not allow for the socket. They ran out of space and so the design stands incomplete, stopping abruptly along an ancient grassline.

The initial placement of the entrance stone at Newgrange was a rough approximation of an astronomical alignment, precisely marked using the simple convention of a vertical groove. This appears as a bold stroke through the design and also occurs on an impressively decorated stone to the rear of Newgrange (K52). Vertical grooves are also found on other structurally important kerbstones in the Boyne valley, appearing in differing positions on the stones and often off centre.

Megalithic art, such as that found in so accomplished a fashion on the entrance stone at Newgrange, is only found in Ireland on passage tombs. This funerary art distinguishes these passage tomb-builders from the other tomb-building communities in Ireland. A key aesthetic component of their ritual practice is a concentration of art on the structural stones of their tombs and grave goods, including pottery and pendants. By applying art to the stones, the passage tomb-builders may have been making their ideology visually permanent in the same way that biblical scenes appear on the high crosses of the Early Christian period in Ireland. The art reflects an ornamental tradition present in a restricted coastal strip along the western edge of Europe during the Neolithic, the origins of which lay in south-east Europe. It does not occur on all passage tombs and is mostly found on the large and more prestigious tombs such as Newgrange. Tombs with the most lavish art are of the highest architectural quality. There are key concentrations of decorated tombs in western Iberia and on the Gulf of Morbihan (near Carnac in Brittany), but the Boyne Valley is pre-eminent. Over six hundred decorated stones in the Boyne represent two-thirds of the megalithic art of Europe and more than four-fifths of the decorated passage tomb stones in Ireland. This art is a sophisticated blend of Irish and overseas influences, transformed by the creative spirit of master craftsmen.

Newgrange is exclusively associated with abstract art and this has provoked much speculation about its meaning. Some suggest that the people who decorated the passage tomb at Newgrange drew on the imagery of ritualised altered states of consciousness … in other words, the stones bear images they saw when they were stoned. If so, one marvels at their ability to maintain these ephemeral visions long enough to recreate such masterpieces in stone. One experiment with hallucinogens produced a pen-and-ink drawing that combined spirals and lozenges uncannily similar to those on the entrance stone. Darkness, cold and silence, even migraine can induce similar altered states. The simple act of lightly pressing your fingertips on your eyeballs can elicit unusual visual effects. Megalithic art and 'shamanistic' art, share a range of abstract shapes and patterns, none of which, however, are imbued with any specific meaning. Once these designs were executed on stone they in turn may have taken a part in Neolithic vision quests. Persistent viewing of the large concentric circles in the chamber induces optical illusions in some, including a sense of entering a vortex.

The meaning of megalithic art is generally dismissed as the puerile pursuit of the pseudo-scientist. Explanations include astronomical and geographical interpretations. Astronomy is foremost in these explanations because of the solstice phenomenon. For example, the cupmarks on the back kerbstone (K52) have been identified as Orion's belt. A geographical reading of the entrance stone sees the three spirals as representing the three passage tombs in the bend of the Boyne, the lozenges symbolise adjacent fields and the wavy lines beneath the spirals depict the Boyne.

Interpretations come in cycles, which often reflect the cultural background of the period: feminism, Freudianism, materialism, etc. Current interpretations, therefore, have more to do with the time we live in than with the Neolithic. It is also impossible to escape the legacy of the drug culture and its attendant interest in mysticism and shamanism. The inconvenient truth is, that in the absence of the original artists, we can never hope to have more than the very vaguest concept of what they were trying to convey.

Technically, the art is characterised by carved and picked designs that are non-representational. Newgrange and the Boyne Valley art in general is exclusively geometric and deploys a limited range of abstract motifs that break down into two main categories: curvilinear and rectilinear. The earliest style is based on a standard geometric vocabulary of circles, spirals, triangles, zigzags and serpentine forms. The art was applied through incision or picking. Incision utilised a flint tool to carve thin lines on the surface of a stone. This technique was used to create guidelines for more complex designs. Picking was the main technique. This involved striking a stone point against the surface to create a small crater (fig. 12). These are then joined together to create larger designs. Some granite cobbles in the entrance façade show signs of wear and these may have been the hammer stones used in the picking. Many stones at Newgrange have been dressed across large areas using this picking technique. This is a very effective technique in concentrating light onto the stone. Each tomb in the Boyne Valley has a repertoire unique to itself: spirals, lozenges and zigzags are most common at Newgrange. The rarest motifs at Newgrange (but common elsewhere in the Boyne Valley), are radiating lines, usually with a central dot in the manner of a child's representation of the sun. Spirals are positioned on the most prominent stones and this is the most common motif in Ireland. In some cases, mysteriously, the art occurs on surfaces that were later hidden.

The tomb took so long to build that an indigenous style of art had emerged between the time Newgrange was started and finished. This stylistic revolution used simple design but created a bolder visual impact. The artists adopted a sculptural approach and were as inspired by the shape of the stones

NATIONAL MUSEUM OF IRELAND

Fig. 12   The stone hammer (right) and stone chisel (left) were the tools of a stone carver. Used together, they created the magnificent art at Newgrange.

as they were by the designs themselves. Known as the 'plastic' style, this art overlies previous art and suggests a revolutionary disregard for earlier iconography. The art became visually dramatic and functional as artist and architect became one. Stones bearing motifs in this 'plastic' style were consciously positioned at critical junctures. The largest and most highly decorated stones occur in the kerb closest to the entrance. Angular motifs on the roof box entice one into the tomb. The passage is most intensively decorated towards the chamber. The location of megalithic art was arranged purposefully within the overall architectural design of Newgrange. This is certainly the case with the entrance stone which so effectively draws one into the tomb. Directly above the entrance at Newgrange and incorporated into the passage structure is another strongly demonstrative stone, forming a lintel for the unique roof box. This is decorated expertly in high relief, with a horizontal sequence of deeply cut paired triangles forming lozenges which taper in size, adapting to the varying thickness of the slab. A raised moulding runs along the upper surface, framing the decorated panel. The whole surface has been pick-dressed to create a fine finish.

Placing highly decorated stones outside in the kerb of the Boyne Valley tombs, and particularly at the entrance, is an exclusively Irish phenomenon within megalithic art in Western Europe (fig. 13). Kerb ornament has been found at other Irish passage tomb cemeteries but is unknown on even the most profusely decorated tombs in Brittany. Here at Newgrange there are

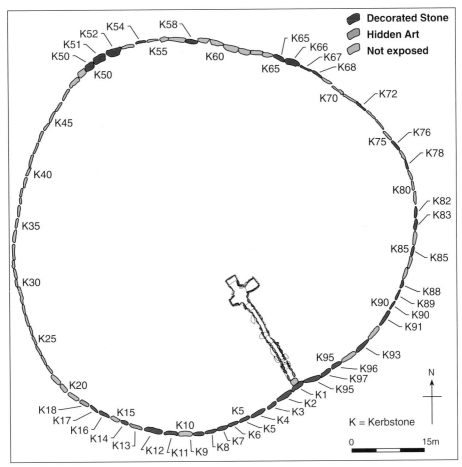

Fig. 13   The occurrence of megalithic art on the passage tomb exterior is unique to Irish passage tombs within the megalithic art tradition of Western Europe (see pages 26-7).

patterns in the placement of the art, with concentrations of decorated kerbstones in particular sectors of the burial mound. There are thirty-nine known decorated kerbstones at Newgrange. Despite decades of archaeological excavations, kerbstones K22 to K47 are still not exposed. We can only speculate about the art that remains to be discovered, but it may not be very spectacular as it is probable that all the stones now hidden were uncovered at some stage in the tomb's history. The decorated stones are arranged in three distinct locations around the mound: at the front façade of the tomb either side of the entrance (K1), coinciding with the limits of the quartz wall; around the highly decorated stone in the north-west side of the mound (K52, fig. 16); and near the third highly decorated kerbstone in the east (K67, fig. 17). Very few of the decorated kerbstones at Newgrange display the quality of design and execution represented by these three stones, which were probably carved by the same master craftsmen. Elsewhere the art can be difficult to see but visibility improves at particular times of the year, depending on the position of the sun shining on the stones. Weathering has been responsible for significant wear and tear on these stones, and many of the motifs are so crude, erratic and indefinite that they may simply be prehistoric graffiti, built up over many years of outdoor ceremonies. They show little sign of being executed by the hands of craftsmen and many people seemed to have been involved. This is in marked contrast to the quality of the kerbstone art at the neighbouring passage tomb of Knowth.

Whereas the entrance stone (K1) at Newgrange is superb, the art on the stones either side of it is unimpressive. For example, the stone to the left (K2) has a simple row of chevrons on the upper face of the stone. The stone to the right (K97), has three faintly incised spirals. Indeed, many of the decorated kerbstones at the front of the tomb display random engravings which are disjointed, isolated and poorly executed. Much of the stone surfaces are left undecorated. In some cases secondary pick-dressing has obliterated the motifs and smoothed many of the natural hollows on the stone.

One of the most perplexing aspects of the art at the front of Newgrange is that the two most highly decorated stones were encased in the body of the mound (K13, K18, figs 14–15). These stones are found at the western limits of the quartz façade and there is no art on their external surface. The back of these stones, however, display an erratic profusion of art. There are concentric circles, crudely drawn spirals, lozenges, zigzag lines, chevrons and hollows. Over one hundred separate motifs are found on each of these stones, thus displaying a complete inventory of Irish megalithic art. Although hidden, this art was dramatic, deliberate and meaningful. One wonders why so much effort was exerted on stones that would have been covered as soon as the tomb was complete. This may have been a conscious decision to hide art that was no longer in vogue, suppressing the iconography of an outmoded religion, but there are other possible explanations. Hidden art is found elsewhere at Newgrange on prominent structural stones. The unseen art may have had just as much meaning for this prehistoric community as the visible art. It has also been argued that at one stage in the construction of Newgrange the kerbstones were freestanding, providing access to both sides of the kerbstones.

Diametrically opposite the entrance stone at Newgrange is the second highly decorated kerbstone (K52, Fig. 16). This kerbstone is located on the north-west side of the mound. Like the entrance stone, it too was carved *in situ* as the pick-dressing ends at a horizontal line along the base of the ancient grassline. This stone had collapsed in antiquity and was reinstated during the modern excavations: the art is vividly preserved. A vertical groove runs down the middle of this stone, which led many to believe that it marked the entrance into a second passage tomb within the mound. However, excavations revealed no second passage here, but there was evidence for a turf mound, which pre-dated the main mound. This stone may have functioned as a 'symbolic exit' rather than as an actual entrance.

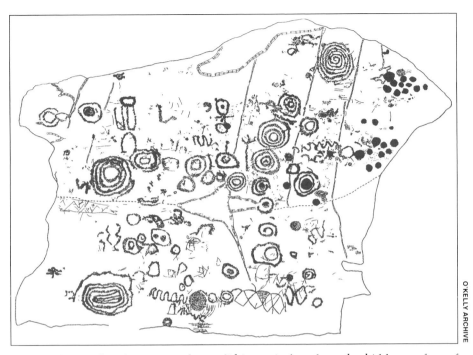

O'KELLY ARCHIVE

Fig. 14   A complete inventory of megalithic art is found on the hidden surface of kerbstone K13, which lies west of the entrance.

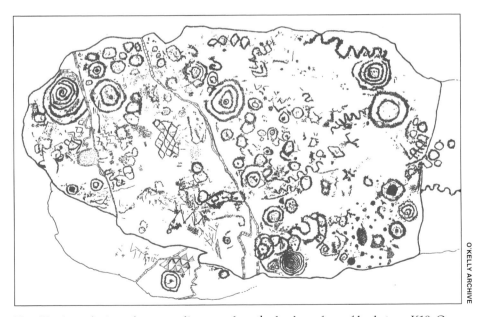

O'KELLY ARCHIVE

Fig. 15   A profusion of art was discovered on the back surface of kerbstone K18. Over one hundred separate symbols were executed on this stone. These motifs were possibly hidden because they represented an outmoded ideology.

CON BROGAN / DofEH&LG

Fig. 16   Kerbstone (K52), the symbolic 'exit stone' to Newgrange, reflects Irish and Breton artistic traditions in its superb carvings.

The broad vertical groove divides the art on the stone cleanly into two parts. That on the left combines two panels demarcated by a natural horizontal fissure in the stone. Above the fissure a pair of double-coiled spirals are set in a clockwise direction. A third, smaller, simple spiral runs in an anti-clockwise direction from them. A lower panel of lozenges has been carved in false relief. Below the lozenges is a zigzag line with triangles beneath. A single lavish design covers the full surface of the right-hand side of the stone. The arrangement of this complicated design was developed around a series of natural hollows in the boulder. Three groups of three cupmarks have been deepened and rounded, and incorporated into sub-rectangular areas defined by double bands. Arranged around these are a profusion of multiple arcs enclosing triangles, some shaped like stone axes. Area-picking extends over the whole surface of the stone and enhances the ornament. The left-hand combination of triangle, lozenge and spiral is an indigenous art style and has many close parallels with the entrance stone. In contrast, the very elaborate design on the right-hand side compares most closely with the art on the megalithic tomb at Gavrinis in Brittany. Here two artistic traditions, Irish and Breton, meet on this magnificent stone.

There is a cluster of decorated stones in the vicinity of this backstone (K52), albeit unimpressive by comparison. There are two stones to the right; one has a faint concentric circle near the upper edge of the stone and two sets of zigzag lines (K51); the other (K50) has a single serpentine motif that terminates in a

CON BROGAN / DofEH&LG

Fig. 17   The placement of this highly decorated kerbstone (K67) in the north-east side of the tomb suggests there is something particularly important happening at this point in the burial mound. The designs to the right of the stone create a face-like impression.

design that can best be described as a stick figure playing football. The second stone has some grouped 'U's incised down its right side (K54).

The last of the highly decorated kerbstones is on the north-east side of the tomb (K67, fig. 17). Again there is a cluster of decorated stones either side of it. Its location is intriguing and the implications are that something particularly important is happening at this point in the burial mound. But like the highly-decorated backstone, limited excavations have failed to identify any significant features here. The design comprises deeply pocked lozenges and triangles on the left-hand side which extend partially around the base of the stone. Immediately to the right is a strongly contrasting design that combines two simple conjoined spirals with two lozenges placed above and below the junction of the spirals. Elsewhere on the stone there are faint traces of other patterns including concentric circles and lozenges. These may have been deliberately obscured when the more elaborate motifs were added. The geometrical motifs create a face-like impression; the eyes are formed by the two spirals, the double lozenge below represents a nose, and the single lozenge represents the forehead. One cannot say categorically that these carvings were meant to be human-like. This effect could be an entirely accidental combination of designs. Neolithic artists were capable of carving accurate depictions of both humans and animals and representational art is a common feature of megalithic art in Western Europe, especially on the Mediterranean island of Malta. Here at Newgrange one is constantly faced with the 'shock of the new', the sophistication of the abstract.

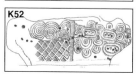

Table 1 – Kerbstones

K1 The highly decorated entrance stone.

K2 A row of chevrons on the upper face of the stone has almost been obliterated by all-over pick-dressing.

K3 A single concentric circle, a dot-in-circle and a cupmark in the lower left-hand face of the kerbstone.

K4 A serpentine and a small panel of joined lozenges, multiple arcs and zigzags. A criss-cross pattern is incised on the right side of the stone where it meets K3. On the back surface are a number of crude devices including concentric circles, boxed chevrons and scratched parallel lines, but there is one elaborate design that combines circles and concentric arcs.

K5 Numerous hollows, some of which have been worked into cupmarks. There are also some very rough circles.

K6 Incised and picked ornament along the base including lozenges, dot-in-circle and rays in circles underneath.

K7 Random picking on top with serpentines, vertical lines and zigzags.

K8 Crude zigzags, circles and spirals on the top of the stone.

K9 Faint zigzags and serpentines.

K11 Various combinations of concentric circles on the back.

K12 Very crude boxed chevrons, some curving lines and indefinite designs on the top surface.

K13 Profusely decorated on back surface.

K14 Faint vertical lines (not illustrated).

K16 A spiral just off centre and some workings on the top of the stone.

K17 A large double concentric circle on the left side of the stone, a triple concentric circle at the top and a double concentric circle on the right.

K18 Profusely decorated on back surface.

K22–K47 Faces not visible.

K50 A single serpentine design with dots.

K51 A faint concentric circle near the upper edge of the stone and two sets of zigzag lines, a fern motif and serpentines.

K52 Highly decorated stone, serpentines on top surface.

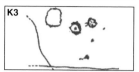

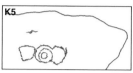

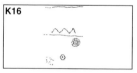

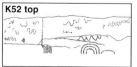

K54 Incised 'U's down the right side, three arcs around circle motif to the left of 'U's.

K58 Circular motif on internal face (illustrated), seven circular depressions on external face (natural solution hollows, not illustrated).

K65 Single spiral on external surface.

K66 Single row of incised zigzag lines above a double row of pocked chevrons, a spiral and large oval spiral on back surface.

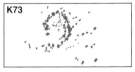

K67 Highly decorated stone of human-like face.

K68 Three circular hollows on exterior (probably natural solution hollows, not illustrated).

K72 Five concentric semi-circles midway along bottom of stone and zigzag line.

K73 Crude oval motif.

K76 Five circles, a crude spiral and two chevrons on top of stone. Two crude circular motifs on back of stone.

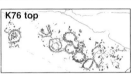

K78 Chevrons on top of stone and two overlapping spirals. Additional crude workings.

K82 Very crude workings, a box-like feature, circular and oval pocked areas.

K83 A circle defined by a broad picked band.

K85 A spiral with zigzag lines.

K88 A row of solidly picked triangles on the top surface and a random arrangement of motifs with zigzags. A dot with picked rays occurs twice.

K89 Vertical zigzags near the right edge of the stone.

K90 Three concentric circles.

K91 A spiral on the right-hand side of the face and a small circle. The back of this stone is decorated with a large design composed of concentric circles and some more erratic workings.

K93 Finely executed pattern formed with long zigzag lines.

K95 Very faint traces of a double spiral and concentric circles.

K96 A random arrangement of a concentric circle, boxed chevrons and other crude workings.

K97 A circle and three large spirals distributed horizontally across the stone's upper face.

(All illustrations courtesy of the O'Kelly Archive except K58, 65, 72, 73, 76, 78 courtesy of Anne Lynch)

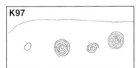

CHAPTER THREE

THE PASSAGE

Nothing that can be written about the passage tomb at Newgrange can capture the experience of ducking one's head down and entering into the dark. The press of tourists, the health and safety warnings, the familiarity bred of countless visits – nothing detracts from this sensation of leaving one world behind and entering another. Thus begins a journey through a space that in its very form mimics the tunnel-like visions of near death experiences. The knowledgeable guides and the electric light can illuminate, but cannot intervene between the modern visitor and their engagement with the distant past. How or why the tomb came to be built, decorated, how it was used and however long ago are less important than the sense of marvel we feel for the work that was done. The same awe applies now as then. We stand as Neolithic men and women once stood.

Just before entering the tomb, visitors to Newgrange cross over the decorated kerbstones into a semi-circular space. The passage mouth is set back from the entrance stone. This space or forecourt is larger today to allow for ease of access, but it was in fact an original feature of the passage tomb and occurs at other tombs throughout Ireland. The original revetment wall would have extended to each end of the entrance stone. One can only speculate on the purpose of this forecourt. It may simply have allowed a space to pivot open the great closing stone. When Newgrange was first discovered the closing stone lay on the ground between entrance stone and the mouth of the passage, causing a considerable constriction. Later it was lowered into place as a great paving slab and one side of the stone was worn smooth from the feet of visitors. The stone, which is only thirty centimetres thick, measures 1.65m high and 1.25m wide. It covers exactly the mouth of the passage and has been re-erected beside the entrance in the open position. In addition to accommodating the closing stone, the forecourt was a place where people gathered before entering the inner sanctum of the burial chamber. Here too the entry of the chosen few into and out of the tomb would have been marked. We witness the same event year after year at the winter solstice with the arrival of government ministers and VIPs.

To enter the tomb, the modern visitor passes into a tunnel of stone one metre wide and 1.5m tall. The first three massive uprights support a capstone 3.7m long. These great capstones are all that lie between you and the tonnes of loose cairn stones pressing overhead. Moving slowly through the passage, individual decorated stones alternate with groups of undecorated stones, the decoration becoming more concentrated as one comes closer to the burial chamber (fig. 18). Key structural stones have been selected for special

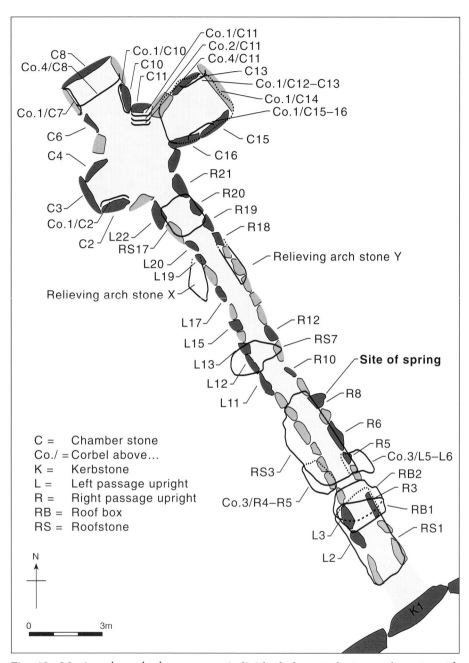

Fig. 18 Moving through the passage, individual decorated stones alternate with groups of undecorated stones but the decoration becomes more concentrated as one approaches the burial chamber (see pages 41–4).

treatment. All of the uprights have a background of pick-dressing which show up the ornament so effectively by reflecting light onto the art.

Fig. 19   A team of workers from the Office of Public Works carefully replaces a massive capstone (RS3), one of the largest in the entire structure, on the roof of the passage during restoration works in the late 1960s. Archaeologist Claire O'Kelly (right) looks on.

At the third stone (R3) we first encounter art within the passage. This stone is decorated at and below floor level with spirals. Beyond the third stone on the right, there is an original gap in the passage that the Neolithic builders infilled with dry stone walling. At this point overhead there is another gap in the capstones and looking up and back one can see out through an aperture above the second capstone. As the passage trends slightly to the right, the ground level starts to rise. In total there is a rise of 1.6m from the entrance to the back of the chamber. The next five stones that line each side of the rising passage support a capstone that is one of the largest stones in the entire megalithic structure (RS3, fig. 19). It is 4m long, 1.8m wide and 0.5m thick. It weighs ten thousand kilograms (over 22,000 pounds). The last stone on the right supporting this massive lintel (R8) is a boldly decorated upright that is a suitable marker of this architectural achievement. It is pick-dressed all over and has panels of horizontally divided lozenges. The lozenges are formed with triangles which have been picked alternatively with a fine and a coarse stone point.

From the end of this massive capstone, the passage trends towards the left and smaller capstones rise up in tiers, like the underside of a stairs, until the passage reaches a height of 2.5m. Here the passage is still a mere 0.9m wide. Megalithic art is present in this restricted section of passage but only as isolated motifs. The exception is the demonstrative art on an upright on the right-hand side (R12). This has three broad, shallow horizontal grooves carved into the lower half of the stone.

At 13.5m in from the entrance, the roof suddenly plunges downward, severely constricting the passage to a height of only 1.4m. At this point the capstone also bears the weight of the massive beehive chamber. From here on, however, the passage keeps rising in height until it meets the chamber, 18.8m in from the entrance. Here we encounter the most dramatically decorated stones of the passage. It is as if the Neolithic artists sought to heighten the expectations of the pilgrims as they approached the burial chamber. The drama begins with one of the more famous and accomplished works of megalithic art at Newgrange (L19, fig. 20). The main decoration at eye-level is a triple spiral with a lozenge in the centre framed by zigzag lines forming a chevron pattern. The carver has carefully pick-dressed around the design to heighten the effect. On the lower body of the stone, there is an S-spiral with two further spirals running off it. Pick-dressing at the base of the stone has partly obliterated earlier spiral motifs. The final upright on the left-hand side of the passage at the approach to the chamber is the tallest stone at Newgrange (L22). It has a panel of wavy bands on the lower left-hand side, defined by a vertical crack in the stone. The wavy bands become more definite at the top of the design as they are transformed into angular zigzags and joined chevrons. Pick-dressing on the surface of the stone avoids this panel of ornament.

At the right-hand side as we approach the chamber, the art is even more exuberant. The second stone from the end (R20) has natural hollows at one edge which have been deepened and surrounded with picked circles. Most of the surface of the stone has been pick-dressed. The final decorated stone on the right-hand side of the passage (R21) is undoubtedly the most atmospheric (fig. 21). It has a sequence of six broad ribs hollowed out across the surface of the stone, all finely pick-dressed. Below these ribs, there is a cavity. When viewed in profile, the shape of the stone is reminiscent of the stone phallus found at Knowth. As one approaches, the edge of this stone has deeply carved oval cupmarks and a sharply defined design of lozenges. Alternate halves of the lozenges are pocked, creating a slightly haphazard design. This stone stands sentinel at the entrance to the chamber.

Here, at the end of the passage, the roofstones are a lofty four metres overhead. Loftier still is the roof of the inner chamber that we have now penetrated. After a journey of squeezing in and stooping down, there is a palpable widening out and a standing up. For the Neolithic visitor this passage must have constituted a ritual humbling before standing erect to finally face whatever deity was deemed to inhabit this inner sanctum.

As impressive as the passage is through which the visitor has come to reach the inner chamber, it is essentially a simple three-sided structure. The chamber offers a whole other magnitude of complexity. At floor level it has a cruciform shaped plan or, put another way, three recesses are built off a common central space. The central area, under the corbelled roof, has an irregular pentagonal shape but it is never less than 2.5m in width. It is an astounding six metres high. The construction of this chamber roof is the

Fig. 20 Ever more dramatic pieces of megalithic art heightened the expectations of pilgrims as they moved along the passageway towards the burial chamber. This fine carving (L19) stands only metres from the chamber.

Fig. 21 The basal cavity and ribbed profile of this passage stone (R21) is strongly reminiscent of the stone phallus found at Knowth. They may have been carved by the same craftsman. The strong 'male' symbolism of Newgrange is often overlooked in New Age interpretations of the tomb's meaning.

Fig. 22   Our familiarity with the corbelled chamber at Newgrange should not blind us
to the remarkable architectural achievement that it represents. It is six metres high. This
composite photograph offers some sense of the vast scale of the chamber.

Fig. 23 A relieving arch carried the burden of the chamber roof over the entrance passage. Hidden decoration was carved on the stones on the left (X) and right (Y).

greatest achievement of the tomb architects (fig. 22). At a height of 2.5m the roof of the recesses and the last great slab over the passage constitute a marked closing in of the chamber roof. Then more gradually, over another ten courses (3.5m), the stones are stepped in, one above the other, until the whole structure could be capped by a single massive slab. The entire corbelled structure was further strengthened with small slivers of stone hammered into the spaces between the roof slabs. The roof has settled downwards as much as half a metre since Neolithic times. This has caused some stones to crack but none has given way and the majestic chamber stands today as it has stood for over five thousand years.

The builders of the tomb were remarkably successful in keeping the interior dry. Prior to reconstruction, a small drip in the east recess was at times heavy enough to fill the basin stone located there. When the excavations exposed the top of the passage tomb, the reason for the dry interior was apparent. The corbelled roof was built so that the stones slanted downwards, running water down and away from the structure. The massive horizontal slabs that capped the passage did not have this natural slope present. In this case, the tomb-builders packed the crevices with a putty made of burnt soil and sea sand. They also cut water grooves into the megaliths to drain the water away. These grooves (5cm wide and 1cm deep) were picked out in the same way as the art executed on the stones and in some cases rubbed smooth with pebbles, sand and water. It was a source of pleasure to the archaeologists

O'KELLY ARCHIVE

Fig. 24   One of the stones used in the relieving arch (Y) shows us how the prehistoric carver, using a series of incised guidelines, laid out a design.

on wet days during the excavation to watch the water run down the stepped corbels and along the grooves provided by the Neolithic masons.

The incalculable weight of the corbelled roof essentially rests on the seventeen slabs rooted firmly in the ground that form the cruciform-shaped chamber. The builders anticipated that the weakest part of the corbelled structure would be where the roof rested on the 'hollow' of the entrance passage. This problem was addressed in an ingenious manner. A relieving arch of three stones was built on the cairn material piled up outside the end of the passage (fig. 23); two slabs rested on the cairn and a third rested on the two side slabs, bearing the weight away from the passage uprights and giving extra strength to this vulnerable area. Significantly, these stones are highly decorated, even though they were always intended to be hidden within the great cairn.

The western stone of the relieving arch is the most profusely decorated. The underside has a seemingly random arrangement of poorly executed concentric circles. There are also some lozenges with less definite workings. Because the stone was protected, the art is as fresh as the day it was carved. This decoration is remarkably similar in style to the hidden art found behind the kerbstones to the west of the entrance (K13, K18). The eastern stone (Y) is ornamented on its western edge (fig. 24). Although the art is unimpressive, it is enlightening in showing us how a design was laid out by the prehistoric

PAUL WOODS

Fig. 25   Persistent viewing of this concentric circle in the left-hand recess is thought by some to induce optical illusions.

carver. The stone is incised with a series of parallel guidelines creating nine panels. The two right-hand panels contain triangles, some pick-dressed, others not. The third and fourth panels have incised triangles showing an earlier stage in the execution of this piece. If completed, none of the guidelines would have survived. This was a work in progress; had it been finished it would have been a stunning piece of art.

As one enters the chamber, the recess to the left (south-west) is the smallest of the three. Its floor area is almost entirely filled with a large (1m in diameter and 30cm thick), roughly circular, hollowed-out basin stone. The face of the left upright of this recess (C2) is dominated by one large, tightly wound spiral in the centre of the stone (fig. 25). Above this there is a panel of lozenges. The corbel immediately above (Co. 1/C2) has a very-well executed linear pattern of lozenges and zigzags. The backstone (C3) is decorated with three single spirals of varying sizes, all set in an anti-clockwise direction. The right-hand side of this recess (C4) has two spirals that are underlined by a single pocked line. At the bottom left is a very unusual pattern which is uncharacteristic and 'foreign' within the art style of Newgrange. This motif is made up of short vertical lines, which are partly enclosed. It has been referred to by some as a 'ship' but we are not persuaded. We are, however, convinced of the fern-like pattern on the edge of this stone facing into the chamber. This is the most naturalistic ornament at Newgrange (fig. 26).

Fig. 26   This fern-like carving on a stone in the south-west recess of the burial chamber is the most naturalistic ornament to be found at Newgrange. The beauty of this carving is marred by nineteenth-century graffiti.

CON BROGAN / DofEH&LG

Fig. 27 Decoration explodes across the surface in splashes of design that are reminiscent of 1960s pop art.

Opposite this, the recess to the right as one enters the chamber (north-east) is deeper (2.75m) and wider (1.9m). There are two basin stones within this recess. The lower stone is a massive, almost rectangular slab measuring 1.8m x 1.4m. Placed on this stone is a smaller but much more finely carved basin of granite from either the Mourne Mountains to the north or the Wicklow Mountains to the south. It is similar in dimensions to the basin stone in the opposite recess but it is thicker and it is pick-dressed all over. Two 'knee-shaped' hollows have been carved near the edge of the basin but, like so much of the passage tomb at Newgrange, the purpose of the indentations is unknown. This is the most intensely decorated of the three recesses. There are many motifs carved into the upright stones forming the recess but most of the art is on the corbels above it. Zigzag lines and lozenges predominate.

The most impressive feature of the north-east recess is the lavish art on the underside of its capstone (fig. 27). Decoration explodes across the surface in splashes of design reminiscent of 1960s pop art. This chaotic composition has at its heart a combination of spirals, lozenges and zigzags that are so typical of the art at Newgrange. To the front and rear of the stone, however, there are two large areas defined by multiple, conjoined arcs which enclose circles in each arc segment. A lozenge forms the centre of one of these motifs, radial lines the centre of the other. The juxtaposition of two distinct styles echoes the backstone and again hints at the merging of two carving traditions. The stone is completely covered in geometric motifs that run into the cairn, proof positive that this stone was decorated before it was put in place. The design,

Triple Spiral Newgrange Tumulus

O'KELLY ARCHIVE

2080

Fig. 28 The triple spiral in the north-west recess has always been recognised as the finest piece of megalithic art in Europe. It was the inspiration for the long-used logo of the Board of Works and also as a trademark for quality Irish goods. This particular postcard was sent to the prominent English archaeologist Glyn Daniel in 1937.

like torn wallpaper, disappears into the roof structure. Its obscure position over the basin stone means that this art spoke directly to the dead.

The third and final recess faces the visitor upon reaching the end of the passage. It is similar in size to the large right-hand recess and it too had a basin stone. This stone is now in fragments due to the zealous efforts of treasure hunters in the nineteenth century. This represents the only significant damage done to the monument between its discovery in 1699 and its being taken into state care. This end recess is singular in its vandalism, but more importantly it contains the single most exquisite carving to be found in the entire corpus of European megalithic art, the triple spiral (fig. 28). This is only fitting when one recognises that this is also the recess that is illuminated on the shortest day of the year, when a beam of sunlight travels up the passage and strikes the backstone.

The spiral is located low down on the undressed surface of the stone that forms the right side of the recess (C10). Because this stone is skewed back, the motif is hidden from the gaze of visitors standing in the chamber. This motif is made up of three double spirals. The two on the right are S-spirals where the ends of the top spiral flow into the bottom spiral. The third double spiral is located to the left centre of the S-spirals. Its two loose ends enclose the spirals to the right. Thus the three spirals are totally integrated into one motif. The designs are picked out in shallow channels which contrasts effectively with the intervening, unworked bands. The isolation and perfection of this single motif makes it a powerful symbol.

L12

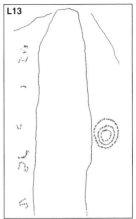

L13

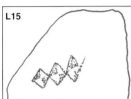

L15

Table 2 – Passage and Chamber Stones

Passage Left

L2 Random pick-dressing (not illustrated).

L3 Random pick-dressing (not illustrated).

L11 A shallow vertical groove down the centre of a stone which is probably natural (not illustrated).

L12 A single pocked chevron near the top on the right-hand side of the stone.

L13 The south edge facing the passage has a pocked S-shaped motif and there are traces of working up the side of the stone that include a chevron. On the northern edge of this stone facing the chamber are three large pocked concentric circles.

L15 A row of three pocked lozenges. These are quartered and the triangles pocked and left plain alternately.

L17 A lozenge is centred on the upper surface of the stone and traces of a concentric circle off to the edge.

L19 Highly decorated stone.

L20 Ornament hidden below present ground level and is very faint; the main element is probably a double spiral.

L22 Panel of ornament on lower left and a double lozenge at centre. The former is defined on the right by a vertical crack and consists of multiple wavy bands of pick-dressing which become more definite at the top of the design as zigzags and joined chevrons. Pick-dressing on the surface of the stone avoids this ornament.

Passage Right

R3 Some random motifs obscured by pick-dressing including two simple circles, an oval enclosing a figure of eight, a fern-like ornament and some wavy lines. Much of the decoration was hidden when placed in socket.

R5 Tiny pendant triangles extend along the upper edge of the stone.

R6 Six deep cupmarks on the south side of the stone, pick-dressing all over.

R8 A panel of horizontally divided lozenges. Both halves have been picked, one with a fine point, the other with a coarse one, creating a contrasting effect. Subsequent pick-dressing.

L17

L19

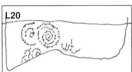

L20

R3

L22

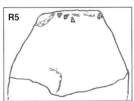

R5

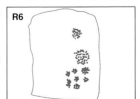

R6

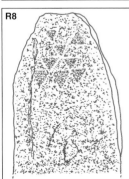

R8

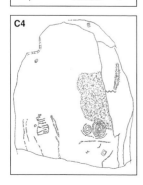

R10 A very simple arrangement of two, poorly executed, joined lozenges in the lower centre of the stone in slight relief. The rest of the stone surface has been pick-dressed.

R12 Three broad, shallow, horizontal grooves cut in the lower half of the stone similar to that on the impressive stone at the entrance to the chamber (R21). There are well crafted rounded ridges in between and the whole surface has been pick-dressed. There are traces of lozenges on an undressed panel beneath these. On the right-hand edge facing the entrance is a series of pocked triangles and above this a small pocked design.

R18 On the upper two-thirds of the stone, an incised and pocked pattern of chevrons, the upper part incised and the lower part pocked on its left-hand side. Below these are irregular markings thought to have been produced by a chisel. Decoration is chipped rather than picked.

R19 A lozenge is picked at the extreme right of the stone.

R20 Natural hollows on the stone have been deepened and outlined with picked circles: most of the stone has been pick-dressed save for a curving line below the top and a narrow ridge that curves downward and to the right.

R21 Highly decorated stone, the most dramatic and atmospheric in the passage.

Chamber

C2 One large, tightly wound spiral in the centre of the stone, above which is a panel of lozenges, both picked and outlined with picking.

C3 Decorated with three single spirals of varying sizes, all set in an anti-clockwise direction. There is a serpentine above the left-hand side spiral.

C4 Two spirals are underlined by a single pocked line in the lower part of the stone below an area of surface picking which partly obliterates one of the spirals. Both adjoining faces are also decorated. At the bottom left is a pattern made up of short vertical lines, which are partly enclosed. There is a very small circle to the left of the pattern. A fern-like pattern is on the east side of this stone.

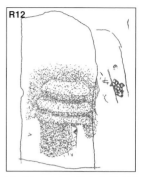

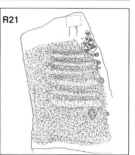

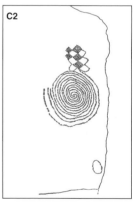

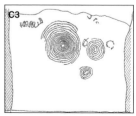

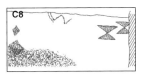

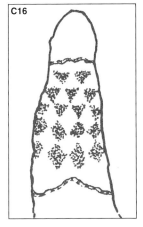

C6 Faint cupmarks in a row near its left edge and vague pocked workings (not illustrated).

C8 A pocked chevron on the upper edge, a zigzag and two sets of joined triangles.

C10 The triple spiral. Above this is a group of faintly incised lozenges in an area. Between motifs is a heavily picked surface. On the southern face of the stone is a simple spiral and concentric circle.

C11 A rough concentric circle.

C13 A series of faint narrow curved bands (not illustrated).

C15 Shallow hollows running down one facet of its surface.

C16 A panel of lozenges and triangles on the uppermost edge

Chamber Corbels
(Course no./Above chamber stone no.)

Co.1/C2 Linear pattern of lozenges and zig-zags.

Co.1/C7 Corbel above the west side of the northern recess. A random arrangement of concentric circles, spirals, semi-radial circles, serpentines and indefinite workings.

Co.1/C10 Two opposing lines of triangles beside a zigzag line.

Co.1/C11 Zigzag lines and a circle.

Co.1/C12–C13 Chevrons, triangles and lozenges. Part of stone obscured by strut.

Co.1/C14 Lavishly decorated underside of the capstone of the right-hand recess with Irish and Breton motifs. Three lozenges underlined by chevrons on the forward edge.

Co.1/C15–C16 Six conjoined surface picked lozenges.

Co.2/C11 Widely spaced surface picked triangles and lozenges.

Co.2/C14 Zigzag and lozenge design that deteriorates towards the right-hand side of the stone.

Co.4/C8 A single lozenge picked on the left-hand side of the stone.

Passage Roof Stones

RS1 Hidden arc of dots around rayed lines and a dot-and-circle.

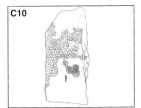

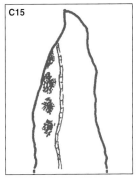

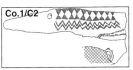

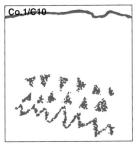

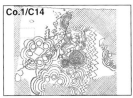

RS3 Hidden widely spaced dots and circles.

RS7 A semi-circular motif made up of multiple arcs on its uppermost (hidden) surface.

RS17 Over the opening to the passage, a series of conjoined triangles which are pick-dressed.

Corbels Supporting Roof Stone 3

Co.3/L5–L6 Dominant design a complex single spiral with concentric circles and serpentines (in National Museum of Ireland).

Co.3/R4–R5 Dot in four concentric circles, polished areas and serpentines (in National Museum of Ireland).

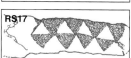

Roof Box

RB1 Lintel with chevrons on outward-facing edge.

RB2 Supporting stone for lintel. Virtually hidden dots, circle-and-dots, a rayed dot and areas of picking. Executed when overlying lintel was in place.

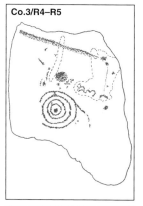

Relieving Arch

X Profusely decorated, hidden art.

Y The 'trial piece', partially ornamented on its western edge.

Z Mere doodles. Found near but not part of relieving arch.

(All illustrations courtesy of the O'Kelly Archive)

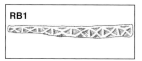

CHAPTER FOUR

THE ROOF BOX

We marvel at the size of the stones and the beauty of their decoration. We marvel at the ingenuity of the Neolithic architects and their precision. We marvel that something that has stood for so long still works. For our Neolithic ancestors to have achieved all this, the totality of the project had to have been envisaged from the outset.

Before the first stone was put in place, before it was literally set in stone, Newgrange was conceived of in the minds of its architects as a monument to the dead and as a solar observatory. The site must have been chosen first. A position in valuable farmland and prominent on the crest of a ridge was chosen. To this day a spring spills out from beneath one of the stones on the right-hand side of the passage (R8). It may have been this object of devotion that led the tomb-builders to the spot. Recent discoveries of a twenty-metre deep well at the Spanish passage tomb of Dolmen De Menga, Antequera, in Andalucia, shows the trouble to which the builders of at least one monument would go to associate their site with water (fig. 54). The site of Newgrange might simply have been chosen for the unobstructed views of the ridge to the south-east over which the winter sun rises on the shortest day of the year.

Once the site was selected, observations were made to establish where the sun rose, the height at which it streamed across the valley and the point where it struck the summit of the hill. This latter point was the most critical because everything at Newgrange was aligned to permit the illumination of the stone that was placed in this position. For all the mysteries posed by this monument, this is our one certainty. Once the location of this backstone was selected, the length of the passage and its ultimate height could be calculated. After this construction could begin.

The tomb was built so that the top of the passage at the entrance is at the same height as the floor of the chamber. One enters the passage and climbs up a rise of two metres before reaching the inner chamber. In our journey up the passage we observed a gap between the second and third capstones of the roof. Now, if we put our faces to the floor of the chamber, we can look down along the passage and out through the gap in the capstones and across to the far ridge. This is the path that the sunlight takes when entering the mound on the winter solstice morning (fig. 29). The kink along the length of the passage channels the entering light into a narrow beam. The precise alignment restricts this phenomenon from occurring more than a few days either side of the solstice.

This makes Newgrange one of the oldest known astronomically-aligned structures in the world, predating the first phase of Stonehenge by one

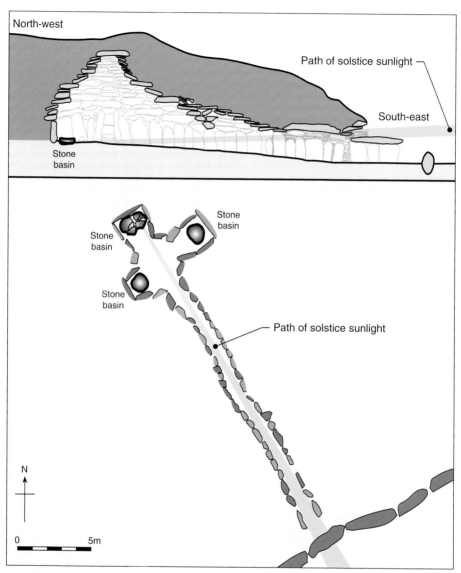

North-west

Path of solstice sunlight

South-east

Stone
basin

Stone
basin

Stone
basin

Stone
basin

Path of solstice sunlight

N

0   5m

Fig. 29   The beam of winter morning sunlight enters the roof box and follows a direct path to the back chamber. The 'wiggle' in the passage narrows the beam before it reaches its final destination.

thousand years and the Egyptian pyramids by four hundred. The alignment of passage tombs with significant solar events is now understood to be a widespread occurrence and is a feature signifying the unified cultural beliefs of Neolithic peoples throughout Europe. In Ireland, ten per cent of passage tombs are orientated on significant astronomical events. A comparable effect is achieved in the chamber at Maes Howe in Orkney where light also passes through the main entrance, an arrangement that has recently been paralleled

O'KELLY ARCHIVE

Fig. 30   Professor O'Kelly (second from right) directs the reconstruction of the roof box at Newgrange, guided by his detailed survey drawings.

at Crantit chambered tomb (also in Orkney), and in Dolmen de Viera (aligned to the summer solstice) in the Antequera group of tombs in Spain.

What makes Newgrange unique, therefore, is not its alignment but the magnificence of the solstice phenomenon that occurs here. This is due to an aspect of the tomb's make-up that was only revealed after the reconstruction of the passage in 1966. The solstice event at Newgrange is made possible by sunlight streaming through the 'roof box', a lintelled structure set back 2.5m from the entrance with a one metre wide, sixty centimetre high aperture that channels the light through the twenty centimetre high gap between the first and second passage tomb lintels. The roof box is a recent discovery and it is also a recent reconstruction. It was as controversial in its early days as the quartz and granite wall (fig. 30).

The roof box lintel had long been visible from the outside of the tomb. Since the 1830s the exquisite carvings along the face of the stone had attracted attention and a good bit of disturbance took place, inspired by the belief that this marked an entrance to another passage. Prior to reconstruction, however, the roof box terminated abruptly where it met the sloping surface of the second roof lintel (RS2).

O'Kelly had the opportunity to study this feature in considerable detail as one of the main reasons for the excavation in the first place was to improve access to the chamber. To achieve this, it was necessary to straighten the first eight uprights along the passage. The roof box and the first three lintels were

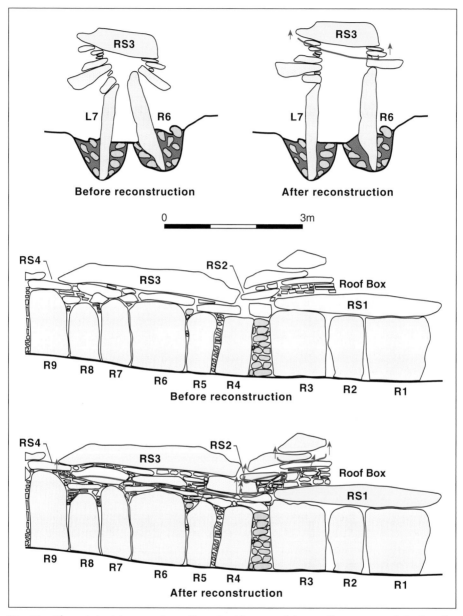

Fig. 31   The original form and startling significance of the roof box emerged during the reconstruction. When the stones of the passage were straightened, roof stones 2 and 3 were raised nearly fifty centimetres. What had been a box became a narrow passage.

removed in 1964 and precisely recorded in each stage of the dismantling process (fig. 31). The first two massive roof slabs rested directly on the passage uprights. Beyond the second lintel, however, the roof slabs rested on layers of smaller slabs that, in turn, rested on the passage uprights. When the passage uprights were returned to the vertical and the smaller slabs replaced, followed by the roof lintels, the third lintel now stood at a higher level than the second and the roof box was no longer a box but a slit providing a narrow access from above the entrance into the tomb. Two quartz blocks were discovered in the roof box during the excavation. These showed signs of wear and there were similar scratch marks on the stone slab that formed the floor of the roof box. This indicated that the aperture was opened and closed at different times over a long period of use.

It would take another three years before the true import of this structure would be understood, but some features suggesting its significance were immediately observed. The bottom stone of the roof box was highly decorated. In addition, two slabs which supported the massive roofstone were carved with motifs always intended to be hidden. These slabs, which helped to raise the roofstone enough to let in the light, clearly had special significance. Like other structurally critical stones, they were carved to accentuate their importance and perhaps as a special blessing for their preservation.

In 1967 Professor O'Kelly made the first observation of the mid-winter solstice phenomenon at Newgrange. What he discovered was of truly stunning proportions and would make Newgrange the best known of all of the world's megalithic tombs. The timing of this discovery could not have been more fortuitous for the future of Newgrange. Just two years previously, Gerald Hawkins had published *Stonehenge Decoded*. It was an international best-seller and it convinced many throughout the world that prehistoric society was more sophisticated than had been thought possible. While the debate raged about the implications of Hawkins' thesis, O'Kelly weighed in with the news that Newgrange was also a precisely constructed and even older observatory of solar phenomena. This too attracted world headlines and the ever-increasing numbers of visitors to the passage tomb every year are testimony to this remarkable and timely discovery.

On the morning of the shortest day of the year, at exactly 8.54 a.m., the sun rises above the lofty horizon of Redmountain, south-east of the passage tomb. The place where the sun first appears is over one hundred metres above sea level, so it has been bright for a considerable time prior to the actual appearance of the sun. Those outside the tomb see the valley alter in appearance under the sun's direct rays; the light, mist and frost combine to paint the river terraces in a fresh palette of pastels. Inside the tomb, those waiting for the rising sun do so in ignorance of conditions in the world of the living. Anticipation is great and there is great doubt too, because it takes only the smallest sliver of cloud to snuff out the phenomenon. Inversely, on cloudy mornings the smallest gap can suddenly appear at the last minute, creating a performance equal to the sharpest and clearest mid-winter morning. One thing that surprises visitors today is that the darkness within the tomb is not complete. Ambient light filters in from the entrance and the outlines of others within the chamber can just be discerned. During the Neolithic, however, the darkness would have been complete with the quartz blocks in place in the roof box and the great closing stone fitted against the passage entrance. When the sun first appeared, the blocks would have been removed and the sunlight finally allowed to stream in.

Four minutes later, at 8.58 a.m., direct sunlight appears on the floor of the passage. It has crossed the valley and entered into the roof box as a horizontal shaft of light. The chamber, being equal in height to the aperture, receives the light. The width of the roof box and the bend in the passage narrows the stream of light to a narrow beam. Its arrival is sudden and to call it sunlight fails to capture the animate nature of the seventeen centimetre wide band of light that penetrates the tomb. Neither is it Freudian to think in terms of phallus and womb as the inner recesses are illuminated by this glowing rod of warm light. Seamus Heaney alludes to this in his poem 'Dream of Solstice':

> … for an eastern dazzle
> To send forth light like share-shine in a furrow
>
> Steadily deeper, farther available,
> Creeping along the floor of the passage grave
> To backstone and capstone, to hold its candle
>
> Inside the cosmic hill. Who dares say 'love'
> At this cold coming? …

The beam of light swims against the sandy floor of the tomb, a rich orangey-red colour that can be seen in a flame but which cannot be reproduced using electric light (fig. 32). Faces suddenly come into view, as does the art in the chamber and the recesses. In Neolithic times it would have been as if a living flame of the sun itself had pierced the tomb, like a blessing across the ashes and offerings to the dead inside. For eleven minutes the light reaches in towards the basin stone of the eastern recess, unadorned except for its exquisite triple spiral, dimly visible in the reflecting light. Then, at 9:09 a.m., the shaft of light begins to narrow and withdraw until, at exactly 9:15 a.m., seventeen minutes after the beam first entered the chamber, it is suddenly ended and the tomb, the observants and the dead are once more plunged in darkness.

The interior of Newgrange may not have been as peaceful during ritual ceremonies as it is today. Tests undertaken at Newgrange indicate that the acoustics are particularly well suited to the frequency of male chanting. Corbelled chambers are ideal environments for producing dramatic sound effects and acoustic features may indeed have been integral to their architectural design. The cave-like interiors of the Orkney tombs were found to have a significant influence on the behaviour of sound. Curved stone surfaces directed echoes towards specific points in the interior of the chamber.

The solstice spectacle occurs in a somewhat diminished form a few days either side of the solstice itself but on these days the light does not penetrate as far into the chamber. O'Kelly believed that the light beam might have been

CON BROGAN / DoíEH&LG

Fig. 32 The winter solstice sunlight reaches the burial chamber, illuminating the innermost recess and its iconic triple spiral.

wider (40cm) when the orthostats at the bend of the passage were in their original perpendicular position. Five thousand years ago, the beam penetrated even further into the eastern recess. Despite these qualifications, and bearing in mind that the event only became possible following the reconstruction of the passage, there can be no doubt that this was the original and authentic purpose of the roof box. This solstice phenomenon brings us as close to the beliefs and sensations of Neolithic peoples as we are ever likely to get.

CHAPTER FIVE

RITUAL

During the Neolithic, a group of people settled in the Boyne Valley who were united by a religious belief and a spiritual vitality that had gripped much of the western fringes of Atlantic Europe. Their religious identity was expressed in their mortuary ritual, a tomb architecture embellished with art, and a particular set of grave goods deposited with the burials. Over the years there have been various claims that the most famous of these tombs, Newgrange, was constructed solely for astronomical purposes and that it is in fact a temple. At the outset it needs to be clearly stated that Newgrange was first and foremost a grave. It was built in the fashion of other graves at the time, which are found across Ireland and Western Europe. Its community followed a strict religious code of practice for burial; a rite of passage set out how the remains should be prepared for burial, what should be provided for the afterlife, and how the remains of the ancestors should be secured within a grand mausoleum.

Newgrange was open for nearly three centuries before excavations began in 1962. Who can tell what was removed from it over those years? To have recovered any original material from the tomb was a huge unexpected bonus for the excavators in the 1960s. Human skeletal remains, burnt and unburnt, representing five adults, were found when the floor of the burial chamber was excavated. This is all that had survived the years of ransacking by eighteenth- and nineteenth-century tomb-raiders. But there had to have been many more humans buried at Newgrange. This is evident in the unprecedented number of stone basins in the chamber, used to contain the bones of the deceased. There are four in Newgrange, more than any other tomb in Ireland. The basin stone in the south-west recess is sub-rectangular, with a flat interior defined by a slight lip; a vandalised, incomplete basin lies in the central recess and there are two in the north-east recess: the lower is rectangular in shape, the upper is a well-finished circular basin (fig. 33). The circular basin is chiselled out of granite and has two circular depressions below the inside of the rim. This basin has steeply sloping sides, flattening towards the centre. The centre of gravity of this last stone basin is located off-centre towards the end away from the circular depressions. This would allow the basin to be tipped up with ease on a hard surface, even by one person. A recent study of the construction of this granite basin shows that the original makers used precise geometric measurements in its creation. These basins are not far removed in size and appearance from saddle querns, which these communities used in their daily life for grinding corn.

The recovered human remains were concentrated near the south-west and north-east recesses and represent spillage from larger deposits originally held

Fig. 33 Within the burial chamber, the right-hand recess was given special treatment by the builders. It is the largest of the three burial recesses, is most handsomely decorated and contains the finest stone basin.

in the stone basins. Even though no human bone was found in the north-west recess, the presence of a stone basin indicates that remains would also have been placed there. Both burnt and unburnt human remains were found within the south-west recess around and beneath the basin, but most human remains were found in the north-east recess. They were badly disturbed and had become mixed with animal remains. Unburnt remains represent two skeletons. One was a heavily-built adult male, between thirty and forty years of age: the other was a more slight and delicate figure of undetermined sex. Burnt remains were mainly fragments of long bones from three or more skeletons; skull fragments originated from at least two young adults judging by the dental remains. The first was aged between twenty-five and thirty-five years and the second was in their thirties. If, as it has been argued, the average age of death in the Neolithic for women was in the mid-twenties and for men in the late twenties, then the deceased from Newgrange were remarkably old. Because cremation was the predominant burial rite in Irish passage graves, the presence of unburnt remains at Newgrange is highly unusual. One wonders if the unburnt remains actually reflect later use of the tomb for burial. The human remains at Newgrange represent a small fraction of the local community and the absence of infant remains could indicate that it was not the practice to bury children in this important tomb. Prehistoric societies had a high infant mortality rate, but because children's deaths normally impact on the immediate kin rather than having any major impact on the social fabric, they tend to be excluded from these mortuary practices. One thing is certain from the finds at Newgrange and from other passage tombs: only a small proportion of the Neolithic population were buried in passage tombs. They must have been the most important members of their community.

A study of the animal remains from the chamber showed that they were not prehistoric. Instead, much of the bone material was made up of animals that had become trapped in the tomb, such as dogs and even a song thrush. The tomb was a warren for rabbits, a refuge for mountain hares, a habitat for bats and a place to hibernate for frogs. The only original remains were seashells brought into the chamber with the sea sand that was used to pack the roof joints when it was undergoing construction.

A seventeenth-century account mentions the discovery of 'some kind of beads' at the first opening of Newgrange in 1699. There is also a 1950s' account of a stone lamp found in the centre of the main chamber, thought to have been used by worshippers in prehistoric times. Excavations recovered a stone lamp outside the entrance to the tomb (fig. 34) and another was found near the bank of the river at Newgrange. Similar stone lamps are known from Iberian tombs such as Anta dos Coureleiros, in east-central Portugal. All but two of the finds from the archaeological excavations within the tomb at Newgrange were discovered in the chamber where the human remains had been laid to rest, rather than in the passage (fig. 35). Thus there is a clear division between the approach and the burial chamber itself. This confirms that the finds are grave goods and part of the actual funerary ritual. There

Fig. 34   Pilgrims lit their way to the tomb in the early winter morning darkness by carrying stone lamps such as these, found outside the entrance to Newgrange.

were only two exceptions to this: a ball or 'marble' made of Antrim chalk had been placed on the socket of an upright on the right-hand side of the passage (R20); a pestle-hammer shaped pendant was found in the centre of the passage floor at the junction of the passage and chamber. It has an hourglass perforation and is made of pottery. Within the central chamber, two stone balls were recovered, made from a dark green rock known as serpentine.

Grave goods were actually found amongst the burnt human bone in the left and right recesses. In the south-west recess of the burial chamber, a maul-shaped, pendant bead made of pottery was found in front of the basin stone. Several fragments of bone pins and points were discovered. The fact that some of these were burnt suggests that they were actually worn by the deceased when they were placed in the funeral pyre. The pins that are not burnt are thought to have fastened leather bags containing the cremated bones.

The right-hand recess produced most of the grave goods found amongst the burnt bone fragments (figs 33, 35). These include a bone 'chisel' similar to that found in Neolithic contexts in Britain, three marbles made from Antrim chalk, a bead, and another pestle-hammer shaped pendant made of pottery. Also found were a barrel-shaped bead and a dumb-bell shaped object consisting of two marbles joined together and carved out of a single piece of chalk with a polished surface. Other than what was found during the excavations between 1962 and 1975, reports of old finds from inside the tomb include an intriguing seventeenth-century reference to a cone-shaped stone with a hole in one end that was observed in the basin stone of the right-hand recess. This may have been a mace head. Once again, the right-hand recess is given special treatment: it is the largest of the three recesses, magnificently decorated, contains the finest stone basin and has produced most of the finds. This focus on one favoured place within the tomb is a feature of many Irish passage graves.

Fig. 35   A strict code of religious practice must have allowed for little extravagance in the goods that accompanied the deceased. The beads are part of a necklace worn by the deceased, but the only items that are grave goods consciously placed with the deceased to accompany them into the next life are the chalk and stone balls, symbols of male fertility.

At first glance the finds discovered within the burial chamber appear unremarkable and even mundane. But they are, nevertheless, typical of the grave goods found in Irish passage tombs built during the Neolithic and must testify to a strict code of religious practice. Ironically, this austere code allowed for little extravagance in the goods that accompanied the deceased to the afterlife, but instead an exuberance in the grave itself. The finds from the burial chamber were mainly items of personal adornment that would have been worn by the deceased. The pendants are tiny miniatures of prehistoric tools. Did they simply reflect tools used by the deceased when they were alive or were they believed to be of some use to the deceased in the next life? The absence of flint and stone tools in the burial chamber was not an accident but rather a standard practice of passage tomb rituals in Ireland. However, an unusual feature in the grave goods found at Newgrange is the lack of any Carrowkeel pottery, a distinct type of crude pottery known from the Boyne Valley, but not from Newgrange.

The only items found within the tomb that are grave goods *per se*, consciously placed with the deceased to accompany them in the next life, are the chalk and stone balls (fig. 35). These are enigmatic objects, thought by some to be representations of testicles. A joined pair of balls was found at Newgrange. The fact that they were made of Antrim chalk suggests that the tomb builders believed this material to have special qualities. If it is correct to associate these balls with male reproductive organs, then it further accentuates the male sexual imagery of the tomb's solstice phenomenon. Such balls have also been found in Iberian passage tombs.

The strict burial ritual practised by the passage tomb builders meant that the finds from smaller passage tombs in the Boyne Valley are very similar to those uncovered from the main mound. This is best exemplified by O'Kelly's discovery of a small tomb, known as Site Z, immediately east of Newgrange (fig. 8). It too was a mound constrained by a ring of kerbstones, but this tomb was only twenty metres in diameter and most of the kerbstones were removed during the middle ages. Finds from the tomb include chalk balls, flint scrapers and bone pins. The most outstanding discovery from Site Z was a highly decorated basin. There were other similarities (in miniature) between Site Z and Newgrange. Two Roman coins, one of debased silver and one of bronze, were deposited beside the largest of the surviving kerbstones. Quantities of quartz were also found. Today the remains of the tomb have been preserved and the sockets of the missing stones are identified by concrete pillars.

Ritual activities must also have taken place during the construction of Newgrange. The hidden art is an indication of this, as was the ritual deposition of decorated stones within the cairn. A remarkable discovery of three decorated cairn stones was made during the excavations of the tomb's overburden of stone (fig. 36). One is a limestone boulder, which combines roughly picked areas with segments of circles and a panel of dots. The second is sandstone with a rough spiral on one face. The third is an intriguing, flattish, water-rolled sandstone with four parallel grooves that run around the edge of the stone and a zigzag on the face. These are instructive in suggesting how designs may have been worked out on smaller stones before being executed on a larger specimen. They may also have had some ritual importance as a component of the hidden art. The flat, decorated sandstone is of huge interest because it is similar to 'portable stones' from megalithic tombs in Iberia. Its four well-cut grooves across one edge are identical to those on the Parafita stone from northern Portugal. A similar stone was found at Knowth. This small stone could help to unfold the mysterious origins of megalithic art at Newgrange.

The religious beliefs of Neolithic peoples were expressed through ritual. Some of the ritual ceremonies at Newgrange were inclusive of the general community and some were exclusive. The ceremonial activity associated with the preparation of the human remains occurred outside the tomb. This would have allowed all to be involved. Prehistoric architects were at pains to provide a fitting venue for outdoor ritual activities. The preponderance of art on the kerbstones indicates that the ceremonies included a procession around the mound, but the poor quality of some of the art on the kerbstones indicates prehistoric graffiti. The main ceremonies must have taken place at the entrance where there is the greatest concentration of art and quartz.

Deposition of exotic stones clearly played some part in the ceremony. Quartz, because of its whiteness, is regarded as a symbol of purity and light in many different societies. In Ireland it is traditionally associated with burials and remembrance. Even today quartz pebbles are placed on modern graves. The cobbles at Newgrange are small enough to have been brought by hand to the monument. Possibly pilgrims from far afield came to these events

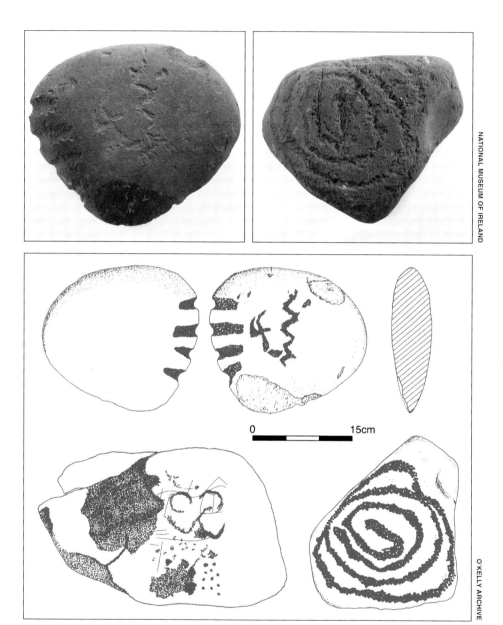

Fig. 36 It was an almost miraculous discovery when the excavation team identified three decorated stones amongst the thousands of tons of cairn material that covered the tomb. A piece of sandstone decorated with a rough concentric device (bottom right) may have been a way of trying out designs or could have had some greater ritual importance as a component of the hidden art. The flat decorated sandstone (top) is similar to portable stones from megalithic tombs in Iberia. It has a zigzag carving on the upper surface and the four chiselled grooves across one edge are identical to those found on a stone from Parafita in northern Portugal. This piece could help to unfold the mysterious origins of megalithic art at Newgrange.

O'KELLY ARCHIVE

Fig. 37   This large dish-like setting was found in front of the entrance to Newgrange. Prehistoric pilgrims placed offerings to the gods in it including quartz, flint and an extraordinary phallic stone.

and left behind a token of their own place. Maybe they even came from the shores of Spain or Portugal and left behind some decorated stones.

Excavations at Newgrange exposed a number of features near the entrance that could be linked to ceremonies associated with burial (fig. 8). An oval setting was found in front of the kerbstone immediately to the right of the entrance stone (fig. 37). A low mound of quartz pebbles and rounded boulders of grey granite covered it. These may have been brought to the tomb as offerings by worshippers. A pavement of flags and cobbles defined this dish-like feature. A flint blade, a flint knife, and a highly polished, 'phallus'-shaped object carved out of sandstone were found on the pavement floor. Foundations of a timber house opening towards the mound was situated to the west of the entrance. A flint axe was found here with a small stone point, a hollow scraper and part of a stone bowl; tools possibly used in the preparation of bodies for cremation and subsequent burial.

The religion of the passage tomb builders was grounded in the landscape and seasonal changes. This farming community had a much more intimate relationship with the earth than we do today. They would have been all too aware of the cycle of the seasons and its implications for their plants and animals, and the changing seasonal availability of food. The ebb and flow of the tides offered a visible rhythm to their daily life. On the land, the turn in seasons was indicated by changes in vegetation and hours of daylight. Important times in the cycle of the seasons were marked by ceremonies at

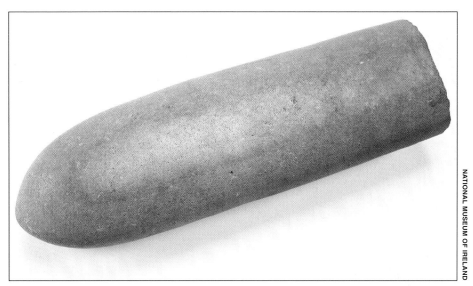

NATIONAL MUSEUM OF IRELAND

Fig. 38 A large, highly polished stone phallus placed as an offering at the entrance to the tomb. It highlights the male sexual imagery of the tomb's solstice phenomenon.

fixed celestial events. The mid-winter solstice was the high-point of their religious year. For the people around Newgrange, the sun coming in the darkness of winter was a poignant sign of the transcendence of life and hope for a new year. Burials were probably placed in the tomb on this day following communal cremation. The passage or roof box was locked into a position aligned to the rising sun on the local horizon. It was fixed on its target. The tomb was built to capture the first rays of the rising sun, to bathe the ancestors with this light, a 'flametide'. They desired that all the community, past and present, share in this annual blessing of the graves.

CHAPTER SIX

LIFE

Today Newgrange sits majestically on a green sward at the top of a natural stairway that ascends from the Boyne river. It occupies the most prominent seat in an island of land enclosed by the curving waters of the River Boyne on one side and the Mattock river on the other. Looking across to Newgrange from the opposite riverbank, one gets a true appreciation of the distinctive character of the area. Here, five and a half thousand years ago, the sea tides ebbed and flowed beneath its feet, and streams and rivers flowed down from Redmountain into the Boyne creating a swirling cauldron rich in the fruits of sea and river, field and forest. Red deer, boar, wild cats and foxes emerged from a canopy of hazel, birch and alder to drink here. A yearly cycle of migrant birds halted here in the Boyne Valley: the whooper swan, water rail, woodcock and pied wagtail. This is a special place, a fitting home for such an extraordinary monument.

To understand Newgrange, we need to know more about the people that were responsible for its construction, and we know a lot about the people who constructed this tomb thanks, in particular, to the pioneering research of Professor O'Kelly and his team of international experts. Michael J. O'Kelly was the father of the 'new Archaeology' in Ireland and the first to incorporate specialist studies into his excavation strategy.

O'Kelly commissioned the leading British environmental archaeologist and author of *Land Snails in Archaeology*, J.G. Evans from the Department of Archaeology, University College Cardiff, to examine the snails found amongst the cairn. Snails are important indicators of different habitats. O'Kelly hoped to reconstruct the original Newgrange environment by using this evidence. Animal remains were examined by Louise Van Wijngaarden–Bakker, from the University of Amsterdam. Her reports were the first published comprehensive archaeological studies from an excavation in this country and she is considered the founder of this discipline in Ireland. During the excavation, O'Kelly also systematically took soil samples for pollen and seed analysis. This provided significant information about how the countryside looked when Newgrange was built.

Various departments in O'Kelly's own University College Cork were called on for expert advice. The Department of Anatomy examined in forensic detail the human skeletal and dental remains found in the chamber of Newgrange. Significantly, O'Kelly produced the first scientific dates for Newgrange using the exciting new technique of radiocarbon dating.

Environmental evidence provided by the excavations at Newgrange offered a profound insight into the natural resources of this area and enables

NATIONAL MUSEUM OF IRELAND

Fig. 39   The stone axe (left) and adze (right) were found outside the entrance at Newgrange. Such implements were part of the Neolithic tool kit.

us to know how it was possible for these early communities to support such a mammoth building project. These were a farming people who understood the richness of the soil beneath their feet. It is quite remarkable that when the mound at Newgrange was sliced open, the excavator noted layers of turves almost as green as when first cut, with mosses, grasses and leaves still clearly visible. Newgrange was built on open farmland, which had been cleared of trees during the centuries that preceded its construction. The mound actually embodies part of that early farmed landscape in its composition, in the form of turves, cereal grains and macroscopic plant remains. Because the soil in the main cemetery area is both fertile and versatile, it would have been suitable for pasture and tillage. Pollen and seeds from a large variety of herbs show that this was an open countryside, strongly influenced by grazing herds of sheep and cattle. The presence of cereal pollen grains in the Newgrange mound demonstrates that the tomb-builders also grew crops. The turves used in the mound came from damp meadows rich in buttercup, blackberry and crab apple, probably from the lower terraces of the river bank. This mixed pastoral and tillage economy, still practised in the Boyne Valley today, was the norm from earliest times. Domesticated cattle, sheep and pigs had been introduced long before Newgrange was built. The animal bone remains from

Fig. 40 An artist's reconstruction of Newgrange and its environs during the Neolithic. It is based on detailed information garnered from specialist environmental reports and archaeological excavation.

the excavations indicate a predominance of cattle over pigs, with sheep and goats also present. There were field fences separating the tillage from the pasture to keep the animal stock away from the crops. They probably used bramble and crab apple as hedging material. The upper terrace below Newgrange has a deep, well-drained soil more suited to cereal cultivation; the lower terrace was probably used for pasture because of the danger of flooding. Heavier soils in the valley of the Mattock river were also good for cattle rearing (fig. 40).

Unlike the tombs, the houses of this community were not built to withstand the ravages of time. These make-shift structures of animal skins and posts would have provided little protection against the elements. Traces of houses appeared during the excavations. Immediately west of Newgrange (beneath satellite passage tomb site L), there was some domestic waste in the form of hollow scrapers and undecorated shouldered bowls. A stake-hole and areas of burning indicated a probable cooking pit. East of Newgrange (beneath satellite passage tomb site Z, fig. 8), a hearth, a cobbled surface and several post-holes appeared. Tools and food remains of the occupiers were also found (fig. 41). They had been working flint and some of the flint waste lay about the place. Again, there were hollow scrapers and undecorated shouldered bowls. The pottery was produced locally and its manufacture was probably 'women's work', as women were involved with food storage, preparation and presentation.

NATIONAL MUSEUM OF IRELAND

Fig. 41 A bone point (centre), chisel (right) and waste flint found in the grave deposits from the chamber at Newgrange. The everyday tools of life found their way into the deposits of the dead.

Before major excavations at Newgrange began in the 1960s, there were some limited excavations around the tomb. These produced a range of stone tools for a variety of domestic activities (fig. 42). Round scrapers were used in the preparation of hides. Blades cut meat or were hafted onto shafts to create weapons. Ten flakes of Antrim flint were found south of the entrance, waste from the manufacture of stone tools. Nearby, a stone adze was found, used for the trimming and shaping of wood (fig. 39). Stone adzes were an everyday tool but they were also used as symbols of power.

These communities successfully exploited the rich soils of their immediate surroundings and took advantage of the long, benign, grass-growing season to rear their cattle and sheep. Local forests provided the hardwoods needed for their house building. Their containers and tools were produced locally. These early communities had to 'shop local' and most of their tools were 'DIY' affairs (fig. 42). Pottery and stone tools are the most likely artifacts to survive from prehistoric settlements. Wood would doubtless have been an important resource but it does not survive in these dry land conditions. Their daily activities would have taken place within walking distance of Newgrange. The raw materials for their stone tools, scrapers, blades and hollow-scrapers

O'KELLY ARCHIVE

Fig. 42 Excavations at Newgrange uncovered the tool kit of a self-sufficient community. Arrowheads (top), such as these examples, were used for hunting. Scrapers (bottom) were used for the preparation of hides.

would have been picked up on the local beaches that lie either side of the Boyne estuary. People travelled by walking or by boat. Many activities took place away from the home such as tool making, hunting and the cleaning of the skins and this is reflected in the presence of flint tools and flint flakes in the ploughed fields around Newgrange.

Some materials, however, came from a greater distance away. This Neolithic community was very aware of the exceptional quality of Antrim flint and it must have been an important trading commodity. Antrim is also where they obtained the chalk used in making the suggestive clay balls that accompanied the deceased in the burial chamber.

Despite the unimpressive nature of their material culture, it nonetheless provided economic support for the major building project that was Newgrange. Food production created a surplus that permitted large numbers of people to be involved in construction for significant periods during the farming year. This society was sufficiently wealthy to permit large areas of turf to be stripped from fertile land and permanently removed from farming. Eventually, they created a landscape that was a reflection of both their farming foundations and their spiritual sophistication. The reality of everyday life was constantly offset against a profound belief in the eternity of their afterlife.

CHAPTER SEVEN

ROOTS

VINCENT: … But you know what the funniest thing about Europe is?
JULES: What?
VINCENT: It's the little differences. A lotta the same shit we got here, they got
    there, but there they're a little different.
JULES: Example?

The character played by John Travolta in the film *Pulp Fiction* was amazed that
two western societies, so similar in some ways, could develop subtle
differences in their material cultures. When asked for examples, he listed
differences in attitudes to intoxicants, policing, even systems of measurement.
Those of us in search of origins for the Neolithic people and culture who built
Newgrange have also been struck by the many close parallels and the many
subtle differences between prehistoric societies in Western Europe.
Newgrange is younger than its continental counterparts by as much as a
thousand years and therefore the culture and inspiration for it came from
outside the island. There are no clear indigenous forerunners. Newgrange is
home-grown but the seed was imported. In the search for an ancestral home,
it is difficult to get a perfect fit. Newgrange is an eclectic blend of Irish and
overseas influences, transformed by the creative spirit of the architect and the
artist. Newgrange also reflects a culture that had matured and transcended its
earlier origins. We therefore have to identify subtle clues in its make-up that
reveal its deeper roots. In a search for foreign influences, we are looking for
communities with a similar religion expressed in the construction of
megalithic tombs and religious iconography, where art played a key role in
burial ritual.

Because of the restricted distribution of megalithic art along the Atlantic
seaboard we are, fortunately, able to narrow down our search. The Neolithic
art of Western Europe is a coastal and island phenomenon and influences
reached Ireland from regions which had a knowledge of the sea and the
sailing skills to cross an ocean. While passage tombs are found in Europe from
Denmark to the Mediterranean, art on passage tombs is known from only four
distinct areas: Brittany, Iberia, Anglesey and the Orkneys (fig. 43). There is a
concentration of Neolithic art in the Paris Basin but, with one exception, this
is not associated with passage tombs. So it is to these four maritime regions
that we should turn to find the origins of Newgrange.

Travelling through southern Brittany (fig. 44) in search of our Boyne
ancestors, one catches glimpses of things that are at once familiar: a cloudy
sky, the ever-changing weather, the omnipresence of the sea, enclosed fields,

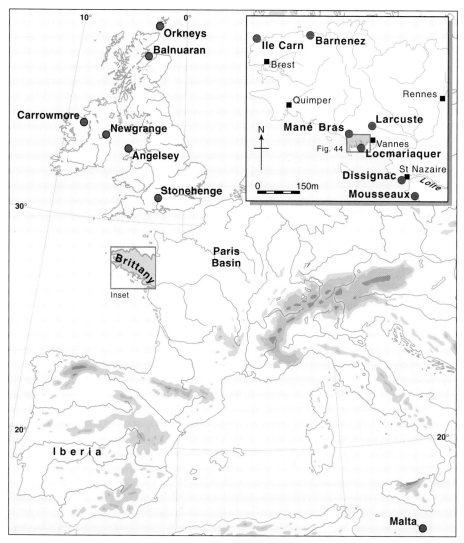

Fig. 43   Newgrange has been influenced by Neolithic cultures from the Mediterranean to the northern coast of Brittany and, in turn, impacted on the Neolithic cultures from Wales to the north Atlantic.

blackberries in the hedges. Communities from here would have felt at home in the Boyne Valley. If we are looking for sources of inspiration for Newgrange, then we must look seriously at this region, not necessarily at one individual monument, but at all the architectural ingredients that make up the Breton megalithic tradition. We are also here because a kerbstone at the back of Newgrange must have been inspired by a Breton carver. Passage graves in Brittany demonstrate a range of architectural features that are found in Newgrange and the Boyne Valley. The earliest passage tombs in Brittany have been dated to *c.* 4,200BC and were being built until *c.* 3,500BC. The cairns are

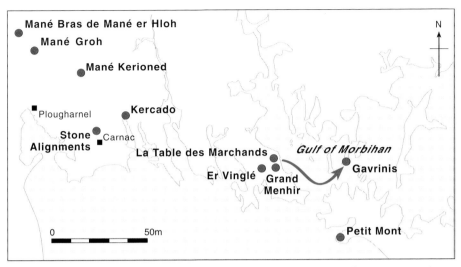

Fig. 44   A distribution map of Brittany showing passage tombs with features similar to Newgrange. The red arrow shows the distance a portion of the Grand Menhir was transported across the sea to Gavrinis.

clearly and deliberately sited, on top of a little hill or on some rising ground to dominate the surrounding countryside. They are generally circular, often flat-topped and (resembling other tombs in the Boyne Valley) two or more passage graves have been placed together under the same cairn. For instance, the tumulus of Dissignac, five kilometres west of St Nazaire, on the mouth of the Loire in southern Brittany, covers two graves, each entered off a passage leading to a central chamber built *c.* 4,500BC. These passages are orientated on the rising sun at the winter solstice. The Breton tomb-builders took great care with the outer surface of the cairns. They did not use large kerbstones, like Newgrange, but they revetted the cairn with dry-walling at their edges and sometimes concentric revetments have been found in the make-up of the inner cairn. The chambers are constructed with dry-walling or uprights or a combination of both. Corbelled chambers do occur, with fine examples on the north Breton coast at Barnenez, but these are greatly inferior to the roof at Newgrange (fig. 45). If we are looking for recesses in chambers good examples can be seen at Mousseaux, near the mouth of the Loire, as well as at Mané Bras and nearby Mané Groh on the Gulf of Morbihan. The cairn of Mané Groh has a passage in the south-east that leads into a space divided into four recesses off a central area.

Brittany rivals the Boyne Valley in the sheer quality and quantity of its megalithic art, with some 250 decorated stones from seventy-five sites, mostly passage graves, which are confined to the coast along the Bay of Morbihan. It has the earliest dated megalithic art in Europe, which has a distinctive form not replicated anywhere else in Western Europe. This earlier art form is representational. There are realistic depictions of yokes and cattle, crooks, hafted axes and bows, along with geometric decoration in the form of

Fig. 45   Barnenez, Finistère, in northern Brittany is made up of two cairns that are revetted with gabion-like terraces. They enclose eleven corbelled chambers but none are as impressive as the chamber at Newgrange. Although often referred to as a parallel to Newgrange, the two sites have very little in common.

triangular and wavy lines, crosses and bell-shaped motifs known as 'bucklers'. This early Breton art is always lightly picked in outline. Massive axes and bows were placed in key positions in the passage to 'guard' the burial chamber. The parochial nature of the art suggests little contact with the world outside its shores.

The exception is the 'crook'. This is an enigmatic symbol when viewed from the perspective of Breton passage tombs alone. But in Portugal the crook also appears on Neolithic structures (although not in passage tombs). The remarkable 'Carnac'-style stone alignments of Almendres near Evora in Portugal have a crook carved on one of the standing stones. These are life-size representations of actual carved schist crooks that *are* known from Portuguese passage tombs (fig. 46). These are ceremonial weapons and must be the origin of the crook used in the Breton tombs as symbols of power.

In its later, more developed style, the Breton art is deeply carved with many images defined by false relief. This art developed out of the earlier form but the motifs have been absorbed and re-worked. This is similar to the much more dramatic and exuberant art style that we associate with Newgrange. It is a style that was to sweep across the western seaboard in the fourth millennium BC.

Take, for an example, La Table des Marchands site in Locmariaquer in Morbihan. It is a passage tomb with the same south-eastern orientation as Newgrange and dates from between 3,900BC and 3,700BC (500 years before Newgrange). Its round cairn is in a dramatic location overlooking the sea. The

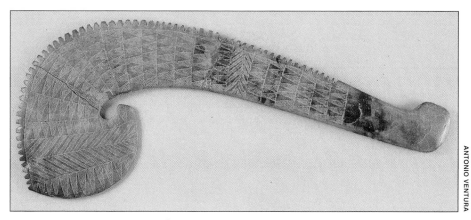

Fig. 46   Angular designs on this magnificent stone 'crook' from the Anta da Herdade das Antas in Portugal look like some of the art at Newgrange. This is the actual object that has been stylised in the art of the Breton tombs.

passage is high enough to allow one to stand comfortably in it and the roof lintels rise one over the other like the underside of a staircase, reminiscent of Newgrange. There are three decorated stones, one in the passage, a backstone in the chamber and a roofstone which is a re-used piece of standing stone known as the Grand Menhir. But it is the massive backstone which is of particular relevance to our investigations (fig. 47). This stone stands out within the tomb because it is formed from sandstone, while its neighbours are all granite. The whole stone has been carved into the shape of a triangle and it has hidden curvilinear art on the back. It is how the art has been arranged on the visible face of the stone that is significant. A blank vertical band runs down the centre of the stone. Rows of crooks picked in relief stand out on either side of this band. This arrangement of the art on the stone is immediately reminiscent of the vertical groove that appears on the entrance and back kerbstones at Newgrange. One wonders if this vertical band also marks an astronomical event in the tomb. The conscious shaping of this stone into a triangle harks back to the presence of a free-standing triangular stone in front of the entrance to Newgrange. The triangular stone here is thought to have been re-used and may have originally been a free-standing 'menhir' or standing stone. Recent excavations have identified the original form of Locmariaquer and a dry-walled retaining wall has been reconstructed around the cairn.

Another Breton tomb, Gavrinis, has many important parallels with Newgrange (figs 48–49). Gavrinis had a short lifespan which ended with the concealment of the entrance, around the time the tombs in the Boyne Valley were being constructed. It is a massive flat-topped cairn located on the highest point of a small island in the Gulf of Morbihan in Brittany. The cairn is delimited by a high drystone retaining wall that flattens out at the entrance in the manner of Newgrange. Gavrinis has a square central chamber and a slightly curved passage orientated to the east. In contrast, the chamber has no recesses. Gavrinis also differs from Newgrange in the absence of kerbstones

71

CNRS / S. CASSEN

Fig. 47 At La Table des Marchands the arrangement of the art on the backstone on either side of a blank vertical band is immediately reminiscent of the rear kerbstone at Newgrange (K52). The 'crooks' provide connections in megalithic traditions stretching from Ireland to Iberia. The carved roofstone is part of the Grand Menhir.

so the art occurs only on stones in the passage and chamber. It shares with Newgrange the presence of hidden art on several slabs. Like Newgrange, the tomb at Gavrinis was re-decorated at some stage in its history; the oldest phase coincides with the classical megalithic art of the Breton tombs, with its catalogue of motifs that included hafted axes, crooks, yokes and horned cattle. It also incorporates part of the Grand Menhir. The later art of this tomb is lavish and immediately reminiscent of the art at Newgrange, albeit in a more oppressive, heavy handed way. Multiple curves and combinations of arcs, chevrons and serpentines cover the surface of the stones. Even the technique of picked lines and the use of false relief is similar. The spiral motif, the 'signature tune' of Newgrange, is present but rare at Gavrinis. The decoration on the stones in the chamber was executed in situ and the ornamentation of each stone in the chamber must be viewed as a unit with patterns crossing over from one stone to the next. This proves that the latest ornamentation was carved when the tomb was fully constructed.

At Gavrinis we see the hand of the master carver in the overall unity of the art work, the unified nature of the designs, the way that they unfold across the stone and in the arrangement of the art in panels using horizontal and vertical lines or natural fractures in the stone (fig. 49). What is familiar is the preponderance of a single motif, the boxed 'U's and individual motifs singled out for special treatment. There is also the familiar repertoire of cup-shaped

Fig. 48   Gavrinis, Morbihan in Brittany resembles Newgrange in having a massive flat-topped cairn, which flattens out at the entrance.

Fig. 49   Gavrinis is lavishly decorated in its interior and is immediately reminiscent of the art at Newgrange, with its boxed 'U's, chevrons and spirals.

CLINT WEIL

Fig. 50   The passage tomb at Kercado near Carnac in Brittany is also surrounded by a stone circle. There is a single standing stone above the entrance to the cairn, which recalls the stone that once stood on top of the mound at Newgrange.

hollows, chevrons and wavy lines. Like Newgrange, all the decorated stones are pick-dressed and the artwork generally covers the whole surface of the stone. The positioning of particular designs in architecturally important places – such as the sillstone at the junction of the passage and chamber at Gavrinis with its line of X-marks – a similar arrangement to the roof box lintel – and the roof slab at the approach into the chamber at Newgrange. And yet the whole is heavy handed, especially when compared to the exquisite understatement exemplified by the triple spiral at Newgrange. The art and culture of the people who built Gavrinis must have influenced the artists at Newgrange, but the Breton kitsch was translated into something much more abstract and sophisticated.

Another site with echoes of Newgrange is Petit Mont, in Morbihan. This enormous multiple-chambered cairn lies on a granite cliff overlooking the sea. A passage opening in the east with an entrance portico leads into a square chamber. The entrance to the chamber was marked by a sillstone containing hafted axe motifs (now in Vannes Museum). Both stones at the approach to the chamber are decorated with rows of zigzags and curving zigzag lines, a motif that occurs frequently at Newgrange. In the chamber there is a stone with a 'rayed sun' motif: a large circle encloses a central dot with radial lines emanating from it. Again, this stone would not be out of place in the Boyne Valley. Serpentines and cup marks occur again and again on stone surfaces in the chamber of this tomb.

Kercado is another impressive site (fig. 50). It is located just south of the Carnac stone alignments in southern Brittany, and is reminiscent of Newgrange in many ways. Ascending breathlessly up a steep incline to reach the tomb, one's mind immediately flashes back to the high ridge above the Boyne. It is prominently sited on a height on the grounds of a chateau, uncomfortably close to a water tower. The eye is immediately attracted to the curving perimeter of the flat-topped cairn with its dry-walled revetment. The circular cairn covers an east-facing passage that leads into a rectangular chamber without recesses. The entrance has a funnel-shaped forecourt leading from the edge of the cairn to the passage. It is dry-walled in the way that Newgrange is thought to have looked. What is most surprising is the presence of a stone circle. The cairn is surrounded by a circle of standing stones like Newgrange (although made of much smaller stones) and there is a standing stone above the entrance on the cairn top. This resembles the eighteenth-century drawing of Newgrange which showed a standing stone on top of the mound. Looking down the passage from the chamber, the eye is drawn to a panel of lozenge-like motifs picked out on the surface of a stone and again one feels at home. Six decorated stones in this chamber contain the earlier Breton art of 'buckler' motifs and hafted axes together with more geometric art that includes ladder-like designs, circles and cupmarks. Excavations produced an impressive assemblage of grave goods that included decorated pottery, axes, green stone beads, schist pendants and burnt human bone. A sample of charcoal from the nineteenth-century excavation gave a radiocarbon date focused on the period between 4,500BC to 4,200BC. The association of standing stones with passage graves occurs frequently in Brittany. We see it again at Mané Kerioned in Carnac.

The passage tombs of Brittany were, like Newgrange, communal graves. Burials have been found every time an unexplored monument has been the subject of a scientific archaeological excavation. However, there is a problem with the preservation of bone remains in this region. The acidity of the soil has destroyed skeletal remains in Brittany where the phosphate in the bones dissolves over thousands of years. In Brittany, cremation does not appear to be as universally practised as it was in Ireland but burnt skeletal remains have been recovered. Collective remains of human skeletons were placed on paved floors in the burial chamber rather than in stone basins. The stone basin has to have been a local innovation and a refinement in the burial ritual of the Boyne Valley.

The Neolithic people of Brittany practiced ceremonies similar to Newgrange. At Newgrange the entrance to the tomb was a focus for ceremonial activity and the megalithic art was concentrated around the entrance façade. The Breton tombs also produce evidence for outdoor ceremonial activity at the entrance to the tombs. Many of the cairns (Gavrinis, Ile Carn and Barnenez), reveal monumental stepped façades used for ceremonial activity, and pottery remains were concentrated on these terraces. Elsewhere, deposits were also found at entrances: in the village of Larcuste, a cairn covering two chambers contained deposits of pottery in front of the tomb; at Mané Bras de Mané er Hloh in Morbihan, hearths were found at the entrance to that passage tomb.

Gazing at the find cases in Carnac museum, there is much that is at once familiar to someone coming from the Boyne Valley. There are miniatures of implements, beads, pendants, worked bone points and spectacular axes formed out of dolerite and fibrolite. These are the same beads that are depicted hanging as necklaces below carved pairs of breasts on stones in the Breton tombs. Pottery is found at most sites (both round bottomed and decorated), along with flint blades and scrapers. What is exciting about the pottery is that it is decorated with many of the motifs that we see on the megalithic art of both Brittany and Newgrange, particularly the chevrons and boxed 'U's. Missing from these cases are the clay and stone balls that are so much a part of the burial ritual at Newgrange.

From this survey many features of the Breton tombs would be at home in Newgrange: including their form, arrangement in the landscape and their association with standing stones. The art is equally lavish and has the same unified approach; it is full of movement, with motifs singled out for special treatment and a shared pool of religious symbols. The techniques of the artist are the same: pick-dressing and false relief. Both communities shared similar outdoor ritual practices and rites of passage. Where they differ is that crema-tion does not appear to have taken place, stone basins are not used and clay balls were not included with the grave goods that accompanied the deceased.

Travelling south to a land that is festooned with modern sun-worshippers, we also find in Iberia an area rich in passage tombs and megalithic art. Isolated on the edge of Europe, facing the Atlantic, it has always enjoyed a close relationship with the sea. It is a land with a tradition of great exploration, especially in the fourteenth and fifteenth centuries, when explorers sailed uncharted water in search of new lands. It too is a region which may have inspired the tomb-builders of Newgrange. The passage tomb communities were more dispersed here than in Brittany (fig. 51). There is less of a sense of a close, symbiotic relationship with the sea and the graves. Here also, round mound covered passage tombs are standard; elevated settings and cemetery groupings are common. There are also similarities in structural details. The large passage graves in the south have corbelled chambers, such as Granja de Toninuela in Badajoz, near the Portuguese border. At Alcalar, near the resort of Alvor in southern Portugal, there is a large, round, flat-topped cairn with a flattened façade at the entrance to the passage (a defining feature of Newgrange). The raised recesses and dry-stone walling at Alcalar are, in turn, also reminiscent of the Orkney tombs.

Iberia has 170 decorated stones from sixty sites, but here angular art is most common. The art also includes realistic depictions of human figures, animals and geometric designs that include 'U's, serpentines, rayed-sun motifs and concentric circles. It is usually carved in the stone but it can also be painted (we have no evidence for painted art at Newgrange). Passage tombs

Fig. 51   Sites in Iberia that have links with Newgrange.

in the north at Castaneira and Barosa have zigzag lines and serpentines like on the stones at Newgrange. Those in southern Portugal have art that would not be out of place in Ireland either, particularly at Granja de Toninuelo, with its depictions of circles, radial lines, panels of zigzags and serpentines.

Fig. 52   This large passage tomb, known as Alcalar 7, located near Alvor in southern Portugal, has been scientifically excavated and has recently undergone an extensive re-construction programme. It has parallels with Newgrange and with passage tombs on the Orkney Islands.

These sites have produced exotic grave goods including schist plaques (fig. 53) and crooks (fig. 46). They are ritual objects placed on the chest or beside the body of the deceased. Angular designs that appear on Iberian megaliths occur in profusion on these magnificent plaques and crooks. These grave goods would have been easy to transport and could be readily carried off to other countries, such as Ireland, where the motifs could be imitated.

Like Newgrange, it is characteristic for Spanish and Portuguese passage graves to occur in cemeteries. Large round mounds cover the passage tombs and decoration is known from several passage graves with large corbelled chambers. Similarly, the tombs in the Iberian peninsula have significant astronomical alignments or are aligned to an important landmark. Iberia too has its large prestigious sites, such as Soto near Huelva in Andalucia, a large circular mound with a long passage that widens into a chamber. All the decorated stones in the passage and chamber are pick-dressed but the megalithic art at Soto is much different from the art of Newgrange. It is much less dramatic, appearing as isolated motifs at different positions on the stones, although there are some familiar symbols, including triangles and circles. This tomb was built after 3,100BC. All the elements of the angular art style at Newgrange could be based on motifs known from Iberia.

One of the most impressive cemeteries in this region with parallels to the Boyne Valley, is the passage tomb cemetery at Antequera, in south-central Spain. There are three colossal round mounds. Cueva de Menga is a massive chamber roofed by one of the largest capstones in Western Europe (fig. 54). It is aligned to an adjacent extraordinary natural rock formation that resembles the profile of a human face. Recent excavations exposed a deep well at the end of the chamber that must have been used in religious ceremonies (this

Fig. 53 A detail from a decorated schist plaque that would have accompanied the deceased in a megalithic tomb in Portugal. Such plaques could have provided the inspiration for some of the megalithic art at Newgrange, where lozenges identical to these are a common motif.

offers a parallel for the presence of a spring in the passage at Newgrange). Cueva de Viera, on the same natural rise, is another round mound with a passage facing south-east, which leads into a rectangular chamber and is aligned with the summer solstice. The third site in the cemetery, Cueva de Romeral, faces south-west towards Menga and Viera. The perimeter of the tomb is revetted with dry-stone walling. All that is missing from these tombs is megalithic art!

The finds from the Iberian passage tombs – axes, beads, flint blades and pottery – are similar to those found at Newgrange. Unfortunately, the magnificent schist plaques are not something we see at Newgrange. Iberian tombs in Estremadura and Alentejo (the region between Badajoz and Evora), have produced stone balls larger than the Irish examples. Comparisons have been made between the highly polished, 'phallus'-shaped object found near the entrance to Newgrange and so-called Iberian 'idols' (fig. 55). These decorated stone phalluses are usually made from chalk and there are good examples from the Lisbon area. Further comparisons have been made between the stone basins at Newgrange and basins found in a small number of Iberian tombs. Iberian sites date from around 4,500BC and are old enough to have influenced Irish ritual traditions.

During the Neolithic both Brittany and Iberia were areas with strong cultural identities and shared religious practices reflected in collective burial in stone-built tombs under round mounds, placed in prominent positions (fig. 55). Ceremonial practices, rites of passage and grave goods seem remarkably similar along the Atlantic façade of Europe. The Breton sites, however, with their coastal distribution, give the strongest impression of a seafaring community. They had a command of the North Atlantic, the same sea that may be depicted in the rolling wave-like decoration on the entrance stone at Newgrange. The density of megalithic structures in the region is

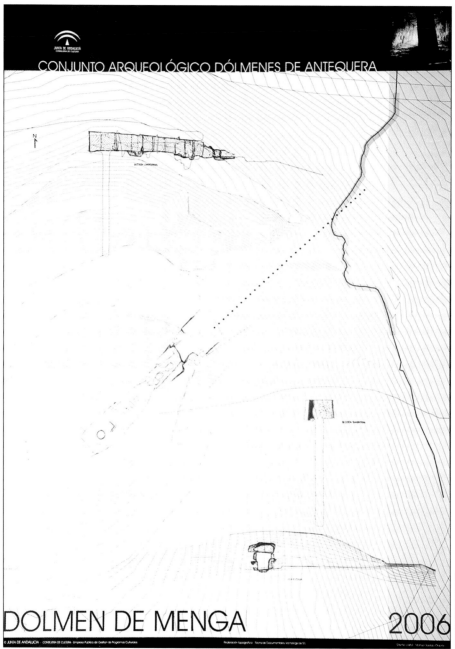

Fig. 54   This attractive poster of Cueva de Menga was prepared for the opening of the new Visitor Centre for the Antequera passage tomb cemetery. A deep well in the burial chamber was, like the spring in Newgrange, a focus for religious ceremonies. The three great round passage tomb mounds that form the cemetery at Antequera in south-central Spain are immediately reminiscent of the Neolithic cemeteries of the Bend of the Boyne. One of these, Cueva de Viera, is aligned to the summer solstice.

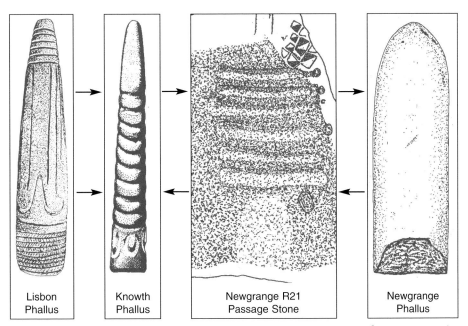

| Lisbon Phallus | Knowth Phallus | Newgrange R21 Passage Stone | Newgrange Phallus |

Fig. 55   Connections between Iberia and Newgrange are seen in the presence of a portable decorated stone, the similarity of some of the grave goods such as the stone balls and the presence of phallic stones found in their tombs. The decoration of the sandstone phallic object found at the entrance to the western tomb at Knowth is similar to Iberian examples and it also like the art on a stone in the passage at Newgrange (R21). A phallic stone was also found in the ceremonial oval stone setting at the entrance to Newgrange.

overpowering. In Brittany, a much more dramatic religious iconography developed from an earlier artistic tradition. The transformation seems to have continued once these traditions arrived in Ireland. If communities in Brittany initiated tomb-building in Ireland, as we strongly suspect, then it began long before Newgrange was built, ensuring that enough time had elapsed for those foreign influences to be transformed into an indigenous tradition.

The evidence so far suggests considerable seaborne contact between communities along the Atlantic seaboard in the fourth millennium BC (figs 54–55). These overseas links were not exclusively continental, nor was it all one-way traffic. Passage tombs with megalithic art are found in north-west Wales and up into the Orkneys in northern Scotland. While communities in Brittany initiated tomb-building in Ireland, communities from the Boyne Valley in turn undertook 'missionary' activity of their own across the Irish Sea and to the Isles of Scotland. There is a remarkable monument on the island of Anglesey that testifies to this seaborne contact. Barclodiad Y Gawres is built on an eminence overlooking the sea on the south-west coast of Anglesey. It is a cruciform tomb covered by a circular mound. There are five decorated stones including both stones at the junction of chamber and passage. The cremated remains of two adult males were found in one of the recesses. Like

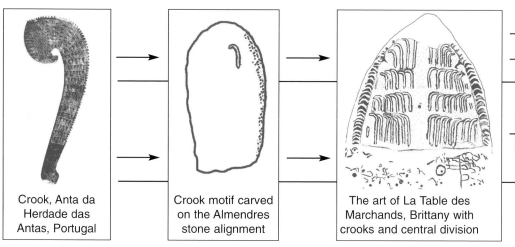

| Crook, Anta da Herdade das Antas, Portugal | Crook motif carved on the Almendres stone alignment | The art of La Table des Marchands, Brittany with crooks and central division |

Fig. 56 A free flow of ideas between Iberia, Brittany and Newgrange in prehistory can be traced in the megalithic art tradition. For example, the 'crook' was a ceremonial object used in Neolithic rituals in south-eastern Iberia. It is carved with geometric motifs similar to those found at Newgrange. 'Crooks' became a common motif in the art of the Breton tombs but there is also a carved crook on the 'Carnac-like' stone alignment of Almendres in central Portugal. There is a 'crook' on the Grand Menhir that was broken into three pieces to form capstones for three megalithic tombs including Gavrinis and La Table des Marchands. It is at Gavrinis that we have the closest comparisons with the art of Newgrange. This link between Iberia and Brittany is translated into Ireland where, although there are no crooks, there are Breton-style curved motifs and the central band is used at Newgrange in the style of La Table des Marchands. Gavrinis also has 'fern-like' motifs, spirals and concentric circles.

Newgrange, they were accompanied by burnt pieces of bone pins. We finally have at this site spirals and plenty of them, and that wonderful combination of spirals and lozenges creating the impression of a face that we have at Newgrange. There are stones covered by a single elaborate design and like the

Fig. 57 The carver of the Pierowall plaque, found on the Orkneys, was inspired by the Boyne Valley art tradition.

82

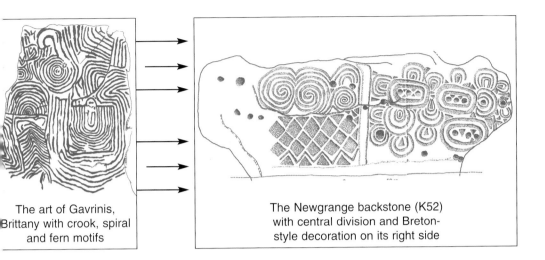

The art of Gavrinis, Brittany with crook, spiral and fern motifs

The Newgrange backstone (K52) with central division and Breton-style decoration on its right side

entrance stone at Newgrange the art spreads across the shoulders of the stone. Another feature noted here is the dressing of the face of a chamber stone where it has been picked back in horizontal corrugations, reminiscent of the innermost decorated passage upright at Newgrange (R21). The backstone of each of the side recesses of Barclodiad Y Gawres bears spiral ornament.

Further evidence for contacts between the builders of Newgrange and communities across the Irish Sea is seen at the Calderstones near Liverpool. These are recorded as having once been part of a large tumulus that was probably a passage tomb. Six structural stones from the tomb have survived and these are all decorated. They have been erected at Harthill, adjoining Calderstones Park. The decoration here consists mainly of spirals and there are concentric circles and cupmarks.

A handful of passage tombs in the Orkneys have produced megalithic art that is similar to that at Newgrange. The iconography includes picked lozenges, zigzags, circles and grouped arcs. A lintel from a site on the island contained a conjoined spiral and circles. At Pickaquoy, near Kirkwall, a decorated stone has cupmarks and concentric circles. The Newgrange entrance stone may have inspired the decoration on a stone fragment found at Pierowall in Orkney. It is exciting to see pieces of megalithic art in the Orkneys that would be at home in the Boyne Valley, and this increases the possibility of direct contact between the two regions during the Neolithic. What is different about the art in the Orkneys is that it is actually turning up in houses and settlement sites. There are incised motifs on the houses in the Neolithic settlement of Skara Brae.

The Neolithic traditions of burial within decorated passage tombs began in Atlantic Europe in the middle of the fifth millennium BC. It continued into the third millennium by which time it had reached Ireland and the outer islands of Scotland. Whatever the origins of these traditions, this culture reached its zenith at Newgrange.

CHAPTER EIGHT

THE GREAT STONE CIRCLE

Professor O'Kelly called it the 'problem of the Great Stone Circle'. He was referring to the uncertain date of one of the most dramatic features of Newgrange, mentioned only now in an effort to maintain a coherent narrative framework (fig. 58). The visitor to Newgrange notices the four gigantic standing stones in front of the passage tomb before he even notices the intricately carved entrance stone. These stones are massive, taller than a human, and broad enough to provide shelter for tour guides on wet and windy days. So why are they a 'problem', why are they not just one more aspect of the remarkable human achievement that Newgrange represents? The answer to this question lies in O'Kelly's perception of the tomb as being purely Neolithic, for it was this pristine exclusivity that he believed set it apart from the other great tombs in the Boyne Valley:

> Newgrange, unlike Knowth and Dowth, was not tampered with throughout the thousands of years of its life. Was this because of its particular association with the chief of all the gods, the Dagda and his son, Oengus?

Unlike the passage tombs of Knowth and Dowth, there is no Early Christian horizon at Newgrange. Here there are no houses or souterrains to turn a sacred site into a warren of domestic occupation. Neither is there evidence for Iron Age occupation nor for Norman fortification. Newgrange *is* special in this regard. But Newgrange is not without evidence for the Early Bronze Age and the most glaring example of this is the testimony of the Great Stone Circle, because the stone circle is a ceremonial monument type most commonly dated to the Bronze Age.

To maintain the illusion of Neolithic purity, it was necessary to date the Great Stone Circle to the Neolithic and to have it feature as a megalithic footnote. 'It may be,' O'Kelly wrote, 'that the twelve stones *in situ* are no more than an exercise on the part of the passage grave builders at disposing of slabs which had been brought on site and which proved too big and/or unwieldy for use in the megalith.' He questions the assumption that there was once a complete circle of stones surrounding Newgrange and he left unmarked the large sockets uncovered during his excavations where the missing stones would have stood. Another inconvenient reality was revealed during the fourteen seasons of excavation, the uncomfortable fact that almost all the finds from the front of Newgrange were of Late Neolithic/Bronze Age date. And yet, as the evidence for a vibrant and innovative period of the site's history mounted

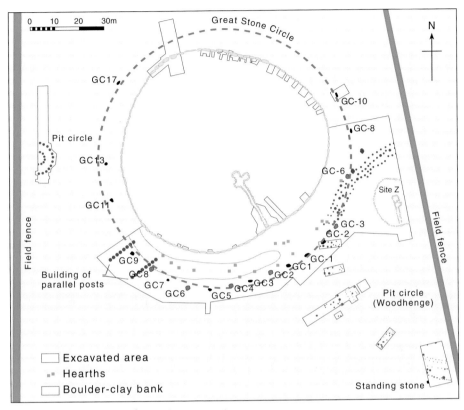

Fig 58   Newgrange in the Early Bronze Age.

up, this occupation remained evidence only of 'squatting', houses were 'unconvincing shelters', a great ceremonial enclosure remained an 'arc of pits'.

The key to the Early Bronze Age at Newgrange was discovered by another archaeologist, David Sweetman. Sweetman, who worked for the national archaeological service, made a contribution to the interpretation of the tomb's history second only to O'Kelly. This story begins not with a grand committee meeting held to decide the future of Newgrange, but with the more mundane aim of ensuring that the construction of a new guide's hut did not disturb any archaeology. In March 1982, Sweetman went out, in essence, to dig the foundations for a new building beside the road in the extreme southeast of the state-owned field. The location of the building was chosen because it was as far away as possible from the entrance to the tomb and hopefully archaeologically sterile. In the cold of an early Irish spring, a team of archaeologists, including experienced trowellers from George Eogan's excavation at Knowth, revealed at first one deep pit, then three pits in a line, followed by an arc of half a dozen pits extending across the full width of the nine metre wide excavation cutting. The cutting eventually yielded-up six arcs of pits and postholes.

Sweetman looked from his rows of pits and posts up the hill to the rows of cement posts left behind to mark the pits discovered by O'Kelly in the 1960s.

CON BROGAN / DoIEH&LG

Fig. 59   A view of the Pit Circle after conservation.

He wondered if they could be the same site. Two trial cuttings proved they were, and another season established the full extent of Ireland's great 'Woodhenge' or ceremonial enclosure (fig. 58). Further, the excavations established the relationship between the passage tomb, the ceremonial enclosure, the Great Stone Circle and the wealth of Early Bronze Age material found near the entrance of the passage tomb. In the light of Sweetman's findings and the reinterpretation of O'Kelly's discoveries, it is now possible to describe the impact of the arrival of a new, sophisticated culture to the area. One clear point remains indisputable, however: Newgrange continued to be the focus of ceremonial activity within the Bend of the Boyne.

We can be 95 per cent certain that the Newgrange passage tomb was constructed some time between 3,370BC and 2,920BC. How long the passage tomb remained in use is not known, but it is impossible to accept that so magnificent a structure was built for a single ceremony. We can also be 95 per cent certain that an enclosure of postholes and pits containing ritual deposits was constructed some time between 2,875BC and 2,455BC. So a gap of merely fifty years, or as many as nine hundred, separates the construction of the tomb and the Late Neolithic/Early Bronze Age activities. It is a frustrating fact, but science can bring us no closer than this to deciphering the chronology of events at Newgrange. Changes came about in part through invasion and conquest (or emigration and assimilation, depending on one's point of view), and in part through the adaptation of a native people to new faiths, ideas and technologies. When the changes did occur, they were swift and dramatic. A new religion came to the Bend of the Boyne, as well as new technologies, and even new livestock. But changes were not so overwhelming or abrupt that

CON BROGAN / DofEH&LG

Fig. 60   Excavation in this cutting showed that the Great Stone Circle was built after the Pit Circle had gone out of use.

knowledge of the importance of Newgrange passed; neither was the passage tomb overlooked in subsequent ceremonies.

This new society constructed the Pit Circle in Newgrange in the middle of the third millennium BC. It was built just nine metres south-east of the main mound at Newgrange, partly on the level ridge-top shared by the earlier passage tomb known as Site Z, but mainly on the steep slope of the south-facing ridge. In its best-preserved sections, the enclosure consists of six arcs of pits, postholes and holes that contained ritual deposits. The outer row of holes held large wooden posts over thirty centimetres in diameter – tree trunks in other words – enclosing an area at least sixty-seven metres in diameter. Inside this were two rows of large clay-lined pits that showed evidence for intensive burning and some contained cremated animal remains. These pits were over one metre in diameter and up to 1.5m in depth, separated one from another by gaps of one metre. Inside the arc of great pits, a further three rows of holes contained cremated remains.

This 'Woodhenge', as it has come to be known, represents a change in religion within the Bend of the Boyne from the exclusivity of whatever secret rituals occurred within the chamber at Newgrange on the morning of the winter solstice, to massive public ceremonies inside huge ritual amphitheatres. A modern analogy for the type of sea-change represented by these developments can be found in the approach to Catholic Mass before and after Vatican II. Before, the priest stood with his back to the worshippers and

CON BROGAN / DoÉH&LG

Fig. 61   The Great Stone Circle by moonlight. This was the last ceremonial monument built at Newgrange.

the mysteries of the altar ceremony were obscured; while the language of the ceremony (Latin) further veiled the nature of the rite. After Vatican II, worshippers had a full view of the altar and of the celebrant. The language used was that of the congregation and the numbers involved in the sacred rite were expanded to include ordinary members of the population. The opening out of religious ceremony in the Late Neolithic/Early Bronze Age represents just such a drive towards greater inclusivity.

Large numbers of people must have come to take part in the ceremonies within this great enclosure. Inside the sanctuary marked out by its ring of stout posts, offerings to the gods were prepared; the finest pigs and cattle, as well as the first horses known in Ireland, were slaughtered. Pottery beakers were ritually smashed in alcohol-fuelled rituals. Fires were lit in the rings of pits within the timber sanctuary and joints of meat were cooked in the open flames. Feasting followed, with the celebration of life and its bounty, in contrast to the more sombre evocation of dead ancestors that ceremonies within the chamber at Newgrange must have evoked. And after the feasting came the ritual deposition of the remains. In the rings of holes inside the line of burning pits a pig tooth has been deposited and, in another hole, a sherd of pottery. Some animal skulls were carried before the entrance stone of Newgrange to acknowledge the presence of this earlier monument to other gods and perhaps to satisfy the needs of those who had gone before.

Another, smaller circle of postholes was discovered during the erection of another building, this time to the west of the passage tomb (fig. 58). It may have been a small (13m in diameter) 'Woodhenge' or ceremonial enclosure, used at the same time as its larger counterpart on the other side of the tomb. The uncovering of Late Neolithic activity here hints at the potential for more

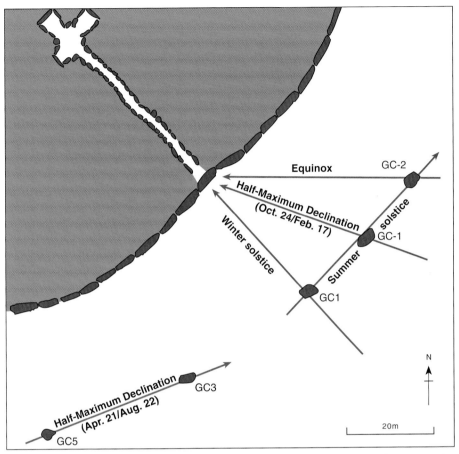

Fig. 62   The stones of the Great Stone Circle act as a calendar casting a shadow on the decorated entrance stone of Newgrange during the winter, summer and equinoxes. This also proves that the entrance stone remained visible into the Bronze Age.

remarkable discoveries in the unexcavated north and western periphery of the passage tomb.

While these ceremonies may seem inconsequential when compared to the solar observations and religious practice of Newgrange proper, subsequent developments showed that the calculation of solar events had not passed out of the knowledge of these people. Some time after the timber circle had gone out of use, the Great Stone Circle around Newgrange was constructed (fig. 60). We know this because a cutting surrounding one of the stones in the circle (GC-2) was re-excavated by both of us while working for David Sweetman (fig. 59). The stone, unequivocally, overlay a pit of the 'Woodhenge'. The construction of the Great Stone Circle was the last act of those who expressed the devotion to their gods by erecting giant stone (megalithic) structures. It also represents the last time that Newgrange was used for astronomical observation and in ceremonies associated with the movements of the sun,

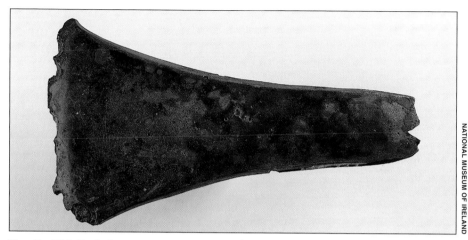

Fig. 63   This Early Bronze Age axe is one of the earliest metal axes used at Newgrange.

moon, planets and stars, until its rediscovery and its modern inclusion in the ceremonies associated with 'New Age' religions. This circle of stones was erected around the passage tomb at a distance of between eighteen metres (in the southeast) and six metres (in the west) out from the kerbstones. The fact that it does not exactly parallel the line of the kerb demonstrates that the Bronze Age builders tried to achieve a greater degree of circularity than did their Neolithic counterparts. Twelve of the original thirty-five to thirty-eight standing stones survive, although fifteen may have been present as late as the 1820s. According to this early account, the only one to record more than twelve stones, 'the present occupier has lately blasted with powder some of these stones that stood in the way of his ploughing'. The surviving stones have not been dressed and there is no evidence for Neolithic 'graffiti' which is a feature of the kerbstones of the passage tomb. If the Great Stone Circle were earlier than the passage tomb, it is reasonable to expect some subsequent decoration. The stones in the circle were between seven metres and nine metres apart. The three at the entrance are the most monumental, reaching heights of 2.75m and widths of 1.5m. There is convincing evidence for the nine missing stones detected during the excavations around the southern perimeter of the tomb. When completed, the stone circle would have been 104m in diameter.

Recent work by archaeo-astronomer, Frank Prendergast, has shown that around 2,000BC the stones acted as a sophisticated observatory. The winter solstice, so important to the Neolithic people, continues as the focal point of this ritual calendar. On the shortest day of the year the rising sun casts the shadow of the stone erected before the passage (known as GC1) across the entrance stone (fig. 61). Similarly, on the morning of the spring and autumn equinox, the shadow cast from the second stone to the east (GC-2) strikes the entrance stone. The alignment of the three surviving stones before the entrance marks the sunrise on the morning of the longest day of the year. Prendergast has identified further alignments that could be used to mark key times in the year for ceremonial purposes and to fulfil the needs of an agricultural society to divide the year into times of planting and times of harvest. This is not an isolated phenomenon. A similar arrangement has been identified at Balnuaran, near Inverness in north-east Scotland, where a passage tomb is enclosed by a stone circle. The passage is aligned to mid-winter solstice sunset. Here, red cobbles were placed among the cairn fill in front of the tomb and these would have glowed in the reflective light. Shadows cast by the stone circle on kerbstones mark events in the solar calendar such as the equinox, thereby acting as seasonal markers.

Professor O'Kelly revealed the staggering extent of activity from this ultimate megalithic phase at Newgrange. There were hearths from houses or shelters, perhaps as many as sixteen, and large quantities of flint, pottery and animal bone. At the west of the tomb there were two roughly parallel rows of large postholes (over a metre wide and a metre deep), indicating that a substantial structure was built over one of the stones of the Great Stone Circle (GC9). When this building burnt down, the fire was so intense that it damaged this standing stone. This may be one more aspect of the ritual activity that took place around the periphery of the great mound. An enigmatic yellow-clay bank was also constructed around the mound on its south-western side but no trace of it was discovered to the east of the entrance. The construction of earthen enclosures was a feature of Early Bronze Age ceremony (many such sites occur in the Bend of the Boyne), but the purpose of this section of bank remains unknown.

Most indicative of the new era that had arrived in Newgrange was the discovery of a metal-working area and an Early Bronze Age axe (fig. 63). The axe, which is similar to the stone version that it replaced, is proof that the people had passed from Late Neolithic technologies into a fully-fledged Bronze Age society. Some commentators on this phase in human prehistory claim that it represents more than just the introduction of new technologies. Some see it as a complete revolution in the way that society was structured. There was a marked simplification in burial ritual that has been interpreted as heralding the emergence of a more stratified society, with a focus on the individual rather than the community. There are feminist and New Age readings of these developments also. Some suggest that the Neolithic society that built Newgrange, and kept it as its ceremonial focus for many centuries, was a utopian, earth-centred, matriarchal civilisation. With the advent of the Bronze Age, the harmonic balance was shattered by aggressive, war-mongering makers of metal weapons. According to this interpretation, they re-figured society into one where males were dominant and the division of labour favoured the new patriarchal order.

We can be 95 per cent certain that no activity at Newgrange post-dates the year 2045BC. For more than a millennium, the tomb had been the ritual focus for one of the most sophisticated societies in Western Europe at that time. Thereafter, for three and a half thousand years the tomb slept, passing out of use, but it never quite passed out of memory.

CHAPTER NINE

RUINS

Newgrange passed out of use but never passed from memory. It is remarkable and impossible to explain, but for more than three millennia a grassed-over mound retained a special significance. During this long span of years, it was seemingly indistinguishable from Knowth and Dowth, the other two large grassy mounds in the Bend of the Boyne. Still it remained the site of the greatest veneration in the Valley, perhaps in all of Ireland.

Newgrange maintained a special place in the minds of those who inhabited the area after the tomb fell into ruins. The firmest evidence we have for this is a collection of Roman artefacts – votive offerings – discovered by chance in the nineteenth century and during the excavations in the front of the tomb (fig. 64). Although the Romans never invaded Ireland, there was plenty of contact between traders from both sides of the Irish Sea and some of these traders came to the Boyne Valley. Knowth may have been an Iron Age fortification at this time, Tara certainly was and everyday Roman artefacts have been found at both sites. The Roman finds at Newgrange, however, are of an entirely different character. Twenty-five coins were found at Newgrange, ten of gold, three of silver. Each of the gold coins was worth at least €150 in today's money, a significant offering! Some coins are as old as 81AD and were minted as far away as Rome itself. Others were minted in London and date from the fourth century AD, from the time when Christianity was ostensibly the official religion of the empire. Coins minted in Cologne, Trier, Amiens and Milan were also found at Newgrange.

The greatest concentration of Roman finds was in front of the entrance and around the three largest surviving stones of the Great Stone Circle (GC1, GC-1, GC-2), that protruded from the mound collapse. There was another concentration of Roman material around the south-westernmost of the surviving stones of the Circle (GC9). Perhaps the Great Stone Circle kept Newgrange a place of particular veneration. No concentrations occur around the sockets for the missing standing stones, indicating that they had been removed during Late Bronze Age or prehistoric Iron Age times. It is possible that these votive offerings were made not by Romans, but by native Irish who had dealings with the Roman world. Claire O'Kelly (Professor O'Kelly's wife and lifelong collaborator) noted in her analysis of the Roman finds at Newgrange that the greatest concentration of valuable coins comes from the third and fourth centuries, a time when Irish raids on Britain assumed their greatest intensity. Nonetheless, we like to think of the finds as those of pilgrims from the Roman Empire taking time out to placate the Irish gods.

In addition to coins other valuable items were offered to the gods at Newgrange that must have had much more powerful personal attachments.

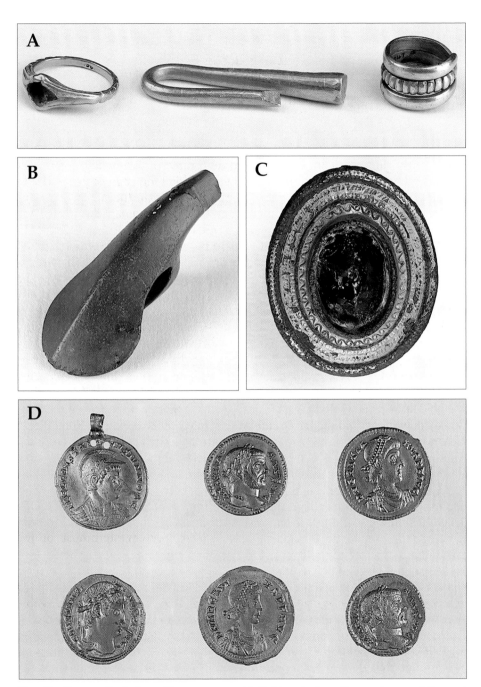

Fig. 64   Roman finds from Newgrange.   A) Gold and silver finger rings and the end of a torc.   B) Portion of a side link of a bronze bridal bit, through which a ring would have passed. C) Disc brooch of cast bronze with a gilded face.   D) Assemblage of gold coins found at Newgrange. These were placed in front of the tomb as votive offerings by visitors from Roman Britain.

There is an exquisite gold finger ring with a narrow band that broadens out to hold a lozenge-shaped stone. There is a ring of silver, possibly a child's. There are brooches, bracelets and glass beads. Each represents an economic and sentimental loss to their owner and each testifies to the widely held belief that Newgrange remained the seat of some supernatural power.

Such ritual depositions occurred at other temple sites and early burial mounds (such as at West Kennet long barrow) in Roman Britain and Ireland. However, the high value of the offerings here is exceptional; Newgrange was an incomparable passage grave because of its solstice phenomenon and unique in that it never became a focus of domestic settlement. The question remains, however, as to the mechanism that kept such a tradition alive down through the three thousand years between the abandonment of Newgrange and the visits by Roman pilgrims. The answer must lie in the rich place-lore (*dindshenchas* in the original Irish) that exists for Newgrange. Ancient legends abound that have Newgrange as their focus. There are stories of kings and battles and miraculous happenings that if told and retold down the centuries would keep the veneration of Newgrange fresh in the minds of each new generation. But there is a problem; according to our surviving Early Christian manuscripts, these stories were only first written down in the late eleventh century. The most rigorous historic practitioners will only allow a text (however antiquated it may seem) to be used to reflect contemporary concerns. In these terms, an eleventh-century tale about a mythological king from a distant past must be read as an analogy for some current (eleventh-century) dispute or as a comment on medieval kingship in general. Others see these tales as 'windows on the Iron Age' (at least), maintaining that they tell of a world so radically different from the time when they were first written that they must represent ancient tales that survived as part of a tenacious oral tradition. Professor O'Kelly was of the latter view:

> Can it have been [Bronze Age people] who planted the first seeds
> of Irish oral literature and should one begin to think of [Irish
> mythology] not as a window on the Iron Age but as one on the
> Late Neolithic?

It is difficult to imagine stories being passed down about a place for over seven hundred generations, but how else can the maintenance of the special place accorded to Newgrange right into the historic period be explained?

In Early Irish mythology Newgrange is Brug (modern spelling Brú) and it had two main functions. Firstly, *brú* is a mansion or a place of hospitality and it was the home of the god Dagda, his wife Boann (the deification of the Boyne River), and their son Oengus (the pioneering nineteenth-century scholar John O'Donovan was first to make this connection). They were of the Tuatha Dé Danann, a people who were thought to have occupied Ireland before the advent of the Iron Age. At one and the same time, Brú is also the burial place of the pagan kings of Tara. One of the tales about Brú recounts how it passed in ownership from father to son. Dagda fell in love with Boann but she was already married and was under the protection of her brother. Dagda arranged that the brother be sent away for a day's journey but it was a day that Dagda magically prolonged into nine months. At the end of this time Boann gave birth to Oengus and in shame abandoned him beside the Boyne. Oengus was rescued by another Dé Danann warrior known as Midir who brought him up unaware of his parentage. Ultimately he learned that his father was none other than the Dagda of Brú and foster son and father confronted the true father at Brú. Midir persuaded Dagda to give Oengus his mansion for a day and a night and then proved to Dagda that day and night follow one upon the other without end. Oengus kept Brú as his own and went on to star in many other heroic tales.

One of the best known stories about the tomb tells of the attempted burial there of King Cormac Mac Airt. In this tale Cormac knows of the Christian god that will come to Ireland in the future. Because of this, he told his people not to bury him at Brú. But his servants were determined to bring him to the place where the kings of Tara had always been buried. They were thwarted in their attempts three times when at each attempted crossing the Boyne swelled up, preventing the bier from crossing. Cormac was then buried at the place still known as Ros na Rí (the wood of the king) on the riverbank opposite Newgrange. The magical manipulation of day and night and the burial of kings are strong themes running through the many tales surrounding Newgrange. It is tempting to think that they are a distant echo of the site's original dual purpose as a burial mound and solar observatory.

Brú as a place name still lingers, in somewhat corrupted forms, but only in the townland that came to be called Newgrange. The field in which the mound at Newgrange lies is called Breo Park and in its immediate vicinity lie Breo House, Breo Lock (on the canal) and the Ford of Brow. The Ford of Brow was still described as such in eighteenth-century estate maps. The fact that all these place names lie within the townland boundary testifies to the antiquity of this territorial unit. It must also mean that the townland was called Brú before it came into the ownership of the Cistercian monks at Mellifont in the twelfth century. Brú only ever applied to Newgrange, never to the general concentration of prehistoric monuments in the Bend of the Boyne, despite modern usage.

The aura surrounding Newgrange certainly saved it from reuse in the long span of years following the Bronze Age, but this did not mean that the tomb did not suffer any harm. Many of the stones of the Great Stone Circle were removed prior to the coming of the Romans. David Sweetman found the shattered remains of a standing stone at the southern limits of his excavation of the 'woodhenge'. This stone had been toppled from its socket and subjected to heavy sledging and was not visible prior to the dig, although it would have originally stood 2.9m tall. It is not known when this destruction took place, but in the Middle Ages trenches were dug along the upper slopes near the tomb and O'Kelly pointed to this activity to account for the destruction of the satellite passage tomb known as 'Z'. Other stones in Newgrange were blown up in the early nineteenth century.

Any damage done in historic times is probably correctly attributed to the Cistercians. They were granted the lands of Newgrange as part of the 20,000 hectare estate of Mellifont Abbey founded in 1142. The Abbey's vast estate was divided into farms known as 'granges' and it was at this time that the ancient name of Brú passed out of general use in favour of Newgrange. These monastic granges were centres of intense agriculture, including grain cultivation, and cattle and sheep rearing. Evidence of ridge and furrow cultivation was uncovered during the excavations on the slopes south-east of the passage tomb and 'plough pebbles', stuck into medieval wooden ploughs to lesson the wear and tear, were also found by Professor O'Kelly. This intense activity must have played a part in the clearing of some of these megalithic obstacles to farming. One cannot imagine the hard-nosed Cistercian farmers paying much heed to pagan legends.

Whatever respect was held for Newgrange clearly waned through the passing years. Perhaps the loss of its original and ancient name contributed to this. Certainly, by the beginning of the eighteenth century, it was merely regarded as a convenient source of stone. This was a time – following the Protestant victory at the Battle of the Boyne – of a great upturn in the Irish economy and newly established landlords sought to improve their estates by building houses and roads. Charles Campbell was one of these Williamite settlers. He received the lands of Newgrange in August 1699 and went straight to work building a mansion, outhouses, coach houses and stables with the stones from the nearby mound. Some time before the middle of December in 1699, after almost four millennia, the passage tomb was rediscovered.

From its discovery in 1699 to the excavations in 1962, Newgrange attracted considerable antiquarian interest and much speculation about its origins and purpose. While many were very wide of the mark, some of the best arguments for its date and function were among the earliest comments. Lhwyd – the first to write about Newgrange after its discovery – believed the site to be 'some place of sacrifice of the ancient Irish' (fig. 65). This supposition was made on the sound (and early) use of stratigraphical evidence; if a Roman coin lay on the top of the cairn, surely the mound pre-dated the empire. There persisted, nonetheless, a strong current of opinion crediting most of Ireland's antiquities to the work of the Vikings, a colonial perspective on Irish capabilities reaching back to the Middle Ages. Thomas Molyneux, writing in 1726, included Newgrange in his book *Danish Mounts, Forts and Towers in Ireland*. In his view, the Irish

> like most nations have been apt to fall into the vanity of deriving
> themselves from a more an[c]ient origin than truth of credible

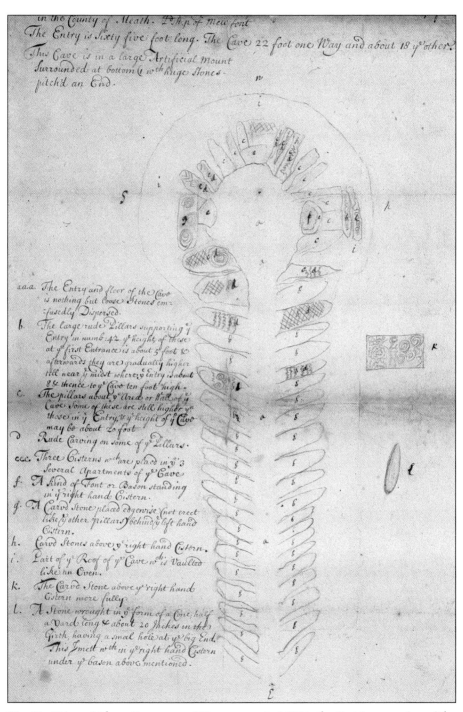

in the County of Meath. Diocese of New font

The Entry is Sixty five foot long. The Cave 22 foot one Way and about 18 ye other.

This Cave is in a large Artificial Mount Surrounded at bottom with huge Stones pitch'd an End.

a.a.a. The Entry and floor of the Cave is nothing but loose Stones confusedly Dispersed.

b. The large rude Pillars supporting ye Entry in numb. 42. ye height of these at ye first Entrance is about 5 foot & afterwards they are gradually higher till near ye midst where ye Entry is about 8 & thence to ye Cave ten foot high.

c. The pillars about ye Area or Wall of ye Cave some of these are still higher yn those in ye Entry & ye height of ye Cave may be about 20 foot

d. Rude Carving on some of ye Pillars.

c.c.c. Three Cisterns which are placed in ye 3 Several Apartments of ye Cave

f. A Kind of Font or Bason standing in ye right hand Cistern.

g. A Carvd Stone placed edgewise (not erect like ye other pillars) behind ye left hand Cistern.

h. Carvd Stones above ye right hand Cistern.

i. Part of ye Roof of ye Cave which is Vaulted like an Oven.

k. The Carvd Stone above ye right hand Cistern more fully.

l. A Stone wrought in ye form of a Cone, half a yard long & about 20 Inches in the Girth, having a smal hole at ye big End. This I mett with in ye right hand Cistern under ye bason above mentioned.

Fig. 65 Edward Lhywd's survey of Newgrange in 1699 is the first known plan of the tomb. It was drawn soon after the passage was discovered.

Fig. 66 This eighteenth-century engraving of Newgrange was included in Edward Ledwich's *Antiquities of Ireland*. It shows the triangular-shaped stone which originally stood before the entrance.

> authority will vouch for; yet no people have carried this extravagance farther than the natives of Ireland.

Edward Ledwich, in his *Antiquities of Ireland* (1790), was convinced that this was a Christian-era monument built by the Vikings for a 'principal commander dying at Newgrange' (fig. 66). Charles Vallencey, who produced the first accurate drawings of the tomb in the 1770s, spoiled his contribution to this debate by suggesting that Newgrange had Chaldean origins (a region of ancient Babylonia *c.* 600BC). It was not until 1806 that an accurate view of the provenance of Newgrange was first described. Colt Hoare, in his *Journal*, first compared Newgrange with sites in Britain such as the Wessex long barrows, a connection still endorsed by modern archaeologists. Knowledge of the tomb must have been fairly widespread at this time because at the end of the eighteenth century a 'Connaught peasant' dreamed that treasure was hidden in the north-eastern recess at Newgrange. Unfortunately for us all, this peasant acted on his dream and broke up the basin stone and dug a large hole in the recess.

William Wilde (Oscar's father) provided a detailed description of Newgrange in his masterpiece, *The Beauties of the Boyne* (1849). He provides a beautifully crafted and accurate description of the passage tomb as it stood a century and a half ago. He looks beyond the native Irish for parallels, but his perceived associations with the Egyptian and Mexican pyramids and the tomb of Agamemnon, though learned-sounding, proved somewhat wide of the mark. Wilde was clearly much taken with the mystery and majesty of the monument. He is apologetic for his scientific intrusion and, we think, secretly in agreement with earlier 'wild flights of fancy':

> When about half lighted up, and we begin to perceive the size and character of this great hive-shaped dome, and its surrounding crypts, formed by stones of such immense size, half revealed to us by the uncertain light of our tapers, an air of mystery steals over the senses, – a religious awe pervades the place; and while we do not put any faith in the wild fancies of those antiquaries of the last century, who would make the world believe that this was a great Druid temple … in which the sacred rites of Paganism, with its human sacrifices, were enacted, we wonder less at the flight which their imaginations have taken.

This antiquarian attention led to early archaeological explorations. In the late nineteenth century, various efforts were made to expose the kerbstones by digging a trench through the cairn collapse and throwing it to the outside, thus creating the present bank and ditch effect which is visible on the unexcavated western and eastern sides of the site. It is impossible to reconstruct the precise history of the works that exposed the kerb; it seems to have been done in a number of stages and in some places repeatedly. A tenant who held the lands of Newgrange did some of this work between 1871 and 1874. The Board of Works, who assumed control over the site in 1882, exposed or re-exposed much of the kerb under the direction of Thomas Deane, the first inspector of Ancient Monuments. No records survive to show, however, whether or not he dug out the full circuit of the kerb. By 1928 the cairn must have collapsed into the trench again because the distinguished (if sometimes over zealous) archaeologist R.A.S. Macalister exposed fifty-four kerbstones, working clockwise from the entrance, until work was stopped by the farmer who leased the land. O'Kelly believes that some further unspecified work on the kerb was completed in 1936. When O'Kelly finished his excavation, however, many of the kerbstones were still not fully exposed. Today, remarkably, twenty-six kerbstones (K22 to K47) are still not exposed.

As more visitors were attracted to the site, more damage was reported to the Commissioner of Works, but nothing on the 'industrial scale' committed by earlier landlords. The year 1890 was the date from whence the modern history of Newgrange commences, for in and around that year three momentous events occurred. The first was the complete exposure of the splendid entrance stone. The second event was the positioning of an iron gate to control access to the passage. The third was the publication of the first modern archaeological treatment of Newgrange and the wider passage tomb cemetery: George Coffey's Royal Irish Academy paper on Newgrange, Dowth and Knowth (expanded and republished in 1912 as *New Grange and the Other*

Incised Tumuli in Ireland). After this publication, an account of those writing on the monument mirrors the prominent names in the history of archaeology in Britain and Ireland and includes Glyn Daniel, Seán P. Ó Ríordáin, Michael Herity, George Eogan and, of course, Michael J. O'Kelly.

Scholars such as R.A.S. Macalister, Robert Lloyd Praeger and Harold Leask continued the work initiated by the Office of Public Works when, in the 1930s, they exposed a further fifty-four kerbstones. Trial excavations by Ó Ríordáin and Ó hEochaidhe in 1956 in the outer stone circle produced some archaeological finds and information on the sockets of the missing stones. Around the same time, Paddy Hartnett discovered flints and an adze south of the entrance, during the laying down of electricity cable to provide light in the tomb (another momentous event in the history of tourism at Newgrange and one profoundly regretted by those old enough to have experienced the passage by candlelight). As Archaeological Officer in Bord Fáilte, the Irish Tourist Board, Hartnett instigated the excavations at Newgrange which were undertaken by M.J. O'Kelly in 1962.

Running in tandem with this scientific approach to Newgrange was the continuous evaluation and re-evaluation of the mystical significance of the place. The Irish Literary Revival (that accompanied the general Gaelic Revival at the end of the nineteenth century), included the rediscovery of the heroic tales of Newgrange. One of the key texts of the revival was the *Heroic History of Ireland*, by Standish Hayes O'Grady, in which the Boyne Valley featured strongly. The excitement of this literary rediscovery is brilliantly captured in George Moore's sardonic (1911) description of the mystically minded A.E. (George Russell) entering the passage at Newgrange, fully expecting to meet there the great pagan god, Oengus. Russell claimed that Oengus was more real to him than Christ. Asked to decipher the strange symbols on the wall of the tomb, he explained to a sceptical Moore:

> The spot within the first circle is earth, and the first circle is the sea, the second circle is the heavens, and the third circle is the infinite Lir, the god over all gods, the great fate that surrounds mankind and godkind.

Russell popularised the concept of the valley as a spiritual centre which modern sceptics might tune into if they dropped their shield of rationalism:

> The palace of Aengus remains to this day at Newgrange, wrought over with symbol of the Astral Fire and the Great Serpentine Power ... The action of this power was symbolised in many ways, notably by the passage of the sun through zodiacal signs.

He believed that the megalithic art concerned an ancient cult in which the serpent was a potent symbol; it was these symbolic serpents of the old religion that the Christian St Patrick had banished from Ireland. Russell was not just some dreamy mystic wrapped in Celtic drapery. Long before the celebrated discovery of the Newgrange roof box by the archaeologist Professor O'Kelly, Russell was somehow, inexplicably, aware of the annual solstice phenomenon at Newgrange, and described it in *A Dream of Aengus Oge* in 1897.

Archaeological excavations did not bring an end to unconventional interpretations of this burial mound but, for some, the excavations lessened rather than enhanced the attraction of the tombs. The painter Nano Reid, for example, stopped painting them after the excavations began in the 1960s. When asked why she had stopped painting in the Boyne Valley, she replied:

> Somehow the place isn't the same since they've started all that excavation. To me the mounds were interesting when you didn't know what was inside them. All the digging reminds me of a curious child who has to tear open a doll to see what's inside and then all the sawdust comes pouring out.

The kind of speculation that the excavations put an end to – like its origins in Celtic times, or its links with Egypt, or its place in the pantheon of Druidic monuments that equally incongruously includes Stonehenge – all this was put at nought again when O'Kelly discovered the solstice alignment. This marks the birth of a new 'New Age' trajectory in the study of the monument, towards the pursuit of prehistoric astronomy. The best known of these works is *The Boyne Valley Vision* (1980), by American graphic artist Martin Brennan. Brennan was a remarkable presence during the period in which he lived in the Boyne Valley. He was a martial arts expert and trained the local football team. Svengali-like, he commanded a devoted following among a dozen or so disciples who accompanied him on his travels. After leaving Ireland some of his library came to our attention and it showed a concerted effort by him to mine the ever-increasing number of monographs, best exemplified by Eric Von Daniken's *Chariots of the Gods* (1968). We still remember the title of one of his heavily annotated books, *The Dragon and the Disc* by F.W. Holiday (1973), and it somehow managed to blend English and Irish archaeology with tales of dragons and flying saucers. Some of these books were, as the term had it in that bygone era, 'far out'.

Brennan claimed that Newgrange was constructed solely for astronomical purposes and that it was not a tomb at all. He attacked archaeologists for their neglect of the crucial astronomical importance of passage tombs, which he described as 'the greatest blunder of Irish archaeology'. His book includes a smattering of Eastern philosophy and displays some detailed knowledge of astronomy. It contains some reasonable observations about the passage tomb art symbolising the moon and sun, and includes some beautifully drawn illustrations, but beyond this the book is barren. His key idea is that an offset carved into one of the kerb stones at the nearby passage tomb at Dowth determines the basic measures upon which all prehistoric monuments in Ireland were designed and located. The key measures said to have been derived from this carving are: A (26mm); B (36mm), which is only approximately the diagonal of a square with sides of A (it is in fact nearer to 37mm); and C (514mm) which is roughly twenty A (520mm) and fourteen B (504mm), although these measures are regarded by Brennan as coinciding. This fuzzy and extremely inaccurate 'discovery' is basically a badly measured version of the geometrical relationship referred to as the 'Golden Ratio'. From this point Brennan's theories are based on matrices of circles and/or lines drawn in unexplained ways but all purporting to be based on his A, B and C measures. These matrices are superimposed on drawings of the stones and these are said to provide elaborate and precise means by which the heavens could be measured and its movements predicted. As each convoluted matrix follows another overlying the key kerbstones at Newgrange, greater sophistication is said to be revealed. But even the matrices as drawn never have a very convincing number of interstices. Lines converge in some circles (for example), cross at the edge of some, bear no relation to others. Brennan's genius, if it can be so called, is in claiming that each outlandish assertion is in fact a discovery. Never does he actually demonstrate how he, or someone during the Neolithic, could take a rod 514mm long, place it up against a stone and tell you the time of day, or the time of the month, or even of the year. Yet assertions spiral out of control, seemingly like the art at Newgrange:

> This diagram shows how the [highly decorated kerbstone 52 at the back of the tomb] functions as a planisphere. The proportions of the stone reflect the proportions of the universe, and, as a working model of the universe, it is capable of being used to make realistic observations, predictions and calculations. It will always be correct in its predictions because it is not dependent on the position of any fixed star …

Brennan claims, among many inconceivable Neolithic achievements, that the builders of Newgrange were able to measure time to the fraction of a second and calculated cosmic cycles of 1,240 years. Why they sought to do this is never made clear.

We archaeologists continue to be amazed that assertions like these remain in common currency. Neither were we impressed by his dismissal of the burial evidence that had been painstakingly assembled from the excavations at Newgrange. 'What does a fucking bone mean?', was the hostile rebuttal to our arguments in favour of the tomb interpretation, a quarter of a century ago in a Dublin pub. Nonetheless, Martin Brennan made some key discoveries and it is a reminder that archaeologists should never dismiss out of hand the weird and wonderful publications that Newgrange inspires. He noted for the first time a significant astronomical event at Knowth and was the first to record that the setting sun lights up the south chamber at Dowth on the winter solstice.

We find it difficult to imagine why farmers of 5,000 years ago were really much different from farmers today. Their concerns may run as far as knowing when the seasons are liable to change and so make planting crops a successful prospect, but seconds or great spans of years could have been of no direct concern. Most of us, now and in Neolithic times (and in the words of Paul Simon) will get most of the news we need from the weather report.

Newgrange is still subjected to a riot of different interpretations. We can learn something from all of them (although many interpretations say as much about their authors as they do about the tomb). For example, artists drawn to the tombs have been able to record subtle gradations of colour which the impassive camera misses. Untethered from the actual, these interpretations soar into speculative realms, which belong to a mystical dimension of the human spirit. A recent, beautifully written and illustrated publication, *Island of the Setting Sun,* offers a thought-provoking merger of the studies of archaeology, astronomy and folklore, to explain Newgrange's significance. The plan of the tomb is compared to the constellation Cygnus and a strong case is made for the passage tomb being a place where the minute movements of the sun, moon and stars could be monitored. We have tried to keep an open mind concerning these theories and they have even inspired one of us to get up at unsociable hours of the morning to observe key astronomical events, while the other has preferred to sleep on such weighty matters.

At regular intervals, too, 'fabulous' 'new' keys to unlock the ancient megalithic code are announced – and are just as regularly dismissed by the archaeologists. Some theories place Newgrange at the focus of 'ley lines' where the earth's energy is said to flow with special intensity. A major ley line has been identified running from Anglesey to St Patrick's Island on the east coast of Ireland, via Newgrange, and then on to the passage tomb cemetery at Carrowmore on the west coast. It has been suggested that a mega ley line connects Newgrange with the pyramids of Egypt (harking back to Wilde's theories, perhaps and is it pedantic of us to point out that a 'line' of this length is in fact an arc?). The argument is that prehistoric communities had already discovered these ley lines and had deliberately aligned their sacred sites along them. Ley lines are therefore punctuated by standing stones, stone circles and burial mounds, and these are power points along a vast grid of natural energy. Newgrange is one of the most potent points within this massive matrix. Ultimately, most archaeologists are scornful of these claims. As the late Bean Uí Chairbre (one of Drogheda's best known publicans) often said: 'the problem with archaeologists is that they have no imagination!'

Not surprisingly, the solstice phenomenon has been celebrated by leading contemporary creative artists. Painters like Nano Reid, Louis Le Brocquy and Jim Fitzpatrick have found inspiration in the movement and mystery of the tomb's abstract art. Poets, including Seamus Heaney, Richard Murphy and

John F. Deane, have focused on the solstice as an emblem of spiritual solace, a sentiment believed to chime with the original intentions of the tomb-builders. Being present at the solstice – whether with the dignitaries and lucky lottery winners on the inside or the scores of devotees who come to watch from the outside – generates a deeply satisfying sense of the long-running continuity of Irish history, and a real sense of communion with a millennia-old cultural force which penetrates to the heart of human history on this island.

Susan Connolly describes the scene outside Newgrange, at sunrise on 21 December, in her poem 'Sunpath'. At the passage tomb the sacred and profane are always jostling cheek by jowl:

Sunpath

The Garda
Stretched out his hand
Over a sea of people
Don't block the way!
Let the sun shine
Into Newgrange!
Like walls of water
We drew aside.

The passage,
A prisoner of darkness
All year long,
became a shining
sunpath.

The importance of Newgrange has long been recognised by successive British and Irish governments. Official protection dates as far back as 1865 when the site was compulsorily purchased by the state and the concerns of the aggrieved owner were voiced in the London Parliament. The Board of Public Works assumed the care of Newgrange under 1882 legislation, and concerned citizens now had a point of contact where they could voice their anxieties about the monument's well-being. Letters to the Commissioner warned that many of the stones were being defaced by 'evilly-disposed', 'brutish-minded' visitors. Tourism seems to have grown to a sufficient size that from this early date it was regarded as a danger to the passage tomb. Some time around 1890 (files for this period in Newgrange's administrative history appear to be missing), an iron gate was erected at the entrance to control access to the passage tomb.

Things had changed significantly since William Wilde (in 1849) recommended 'Slane hotel' as the 'very desirable residence' from which to visit the Bend of the Boyne. One gets the impression that Wilde was ploughing virgin soil here and that the tourist routes, already so deeply established in Kerry, had only shallow beginnings in eastern Ireland. A survey of over one hundred travellers' accounts of Ireland reveals that only twenty-two concerned themselves with visits to north Leinster. Further, few of the visitors to the area between Drogheda and Slane bothered to visit Newgrange, most confining their sojourn to a pilgrimage to the Obelisk commemorating the Battle of the Boyne. In 1796, a French visitor, Chevalier de Latocnaye, actually walked between Drogheda and Slane without detouring a mere two kilometres to see the passage tomb.

Visiting Newgrange in the nineteenth and in the first half of the last century was not the antiseptic experience that it is today. For a start, the road between Slane and Drogheda was described, in 1837, as 'the very worst I ever was doomed to cross even in the most rugged North American districts'. Access was seriously constricted by the fallen 'closing stone'. A German visitor, in 1842, found it necessary to remove his clothes before entering!:

> … we had provided ourselves with lights, the entrance being extremely narrow and rather long. Before the entrance there is a little space protected from the wind, a kind of cave in the earth heaped up at the foot of the mound and which was probably formed by the explorers and excavators of the entrance. Here we took off our clothes, lighted our candles and commenced our operations. The passage, which is about fifty feet long, is somewhat obstructed with stone, so that one can only work his way in by lying on his back, while he feels his way with his feet, and pushes himself forward with his hands. As the ground is covered with sharp-cornered flint-stones, this slide-path is not the most agreeable in the world.

Then, about one-third of the way down the passage, struts and inward leaning uprights presented a serious constriction. A short crawl upon hands and knees was necessary in this section.

An important year in the history of tourism at Newgrange is 1896, when the Great Northern Railway initiated their 'Grand Circular Tour' of the Boyne Valley. A *charabanc* met the morning train from Dublin and the day-trippers were taken to the passage tombs of Dowth and Newgrange. By 1932 the *charabanc* was replaced by a bus. The train trip was bypassed in the following year with the Great Northern Omnibus Service, which charged ten shillings for an 'all motor coach tour from Dublin'. Increasingly, the private car became the dominant means by which tourists visited Newgrange. A day trip to the tomb via hired motor car is described in a traveller's account as early as 1906.

Despite ever increasing tourist numbers (fig. 67), even into the 1960s prior to the work of O'Kelly, entering Newgrange remained a great adventure. Liam Mac Uistin described the experience in his excellent (1999) guide to Newgrange:

Fig. 67   This 1950s' newspaper photo shows visitors queuing outside Newgrange.

> After some hazardous scaling of walls and fences I found the custodian of the site, an elderly lady [Mrs Anne Hickey] who lived in a nearby cottage. Armed with a few candle stubs, and wearing a leather apron as protection against drips of candle grease, she escorted me to the entrance of the mound and led me inside. By the flickering candlelight the interior began to be revealed. Huge stone slabs, engraved with strange designs, loomed out of the darkness. The further I ventured along the passage the more I felt the macabre enchantment of this cold, silent, secretive place wrapping itself around me.

It is often said that rural electrification sounded the death knell to the Irish faeries. Just as the imagination bred from the dark, the night and the glow of the hearth was their breeding ground in Ireland before the 1930s. Something similar occurred at Newgrange when electrification arrived there late in the 1950s: the mystery evaporated and with it part of the connection between the modern visitor and the Neolithic. Of course, electrification was a response to increased visitor numbers who now, after the retirement of that 'elderly lady' (after at least thirty-nine years, some time after her seventy-fifth birthday), were escorted into the tomb by Michael Smyth, caretaker at Newgrange until 1982.

The better-heeled and more dedicated visitors to Newgrange continued to base their trip in the Conyngham Arms in the nearby village of Slane. Wilde stayed there and it is from 'Mrs Macken's hospitable inn' that Glyn Daniel wrote his moving preface to *New Grange* (1964), lamenting the untimely death of Professor Seán P. Ó Ríordáin. M.J. O'Kelly also stayed in this notable Slane hotel with his wife Claire and his student assistants during the long summers of excavation and reconstruction at Newgrange. The poor quality of the students' food is the most enduring memory of those who stayed at the hotel

Fig. 68 The tourist experience at Newgrange changed markedly after the reconstruction of the site in the early 1970s.

over forty years ago. As is still the case, most visitors in the 1960s came by car or bus and only for a fleeting visit.

A small museum was erected at Newgrange prior to 1964 and run by the local tourist office. Increased visitor numbers in the 1960s meant that tour guides had to be employed to assist the caretaker in the management of the site. David Sweetman, who went on to change our understanding of the site, worked as a guide in the summer of 1968 (he had a row that summer with Professor O'Kelly about accepting tips). In the last year of Michael Smyth's tenure as caretaker of the monument in 1982, there were 75,000 visitors to Newgrange. At this point crowd management became a serious issue, especially in the summer when tour buses and cars caused gridlock in the narrow road below the passage grave. It could also be an uncomfortable time for the guides when, on exceptionally busy days, they had to close the gate in the faces of those seeking entry. In 1991 there was some small relief to the visitor crush when the nearby passage tomb at Knowth was finally open to visitors after thirty years of excavation.

Similar problems were being experienced at Stonehenge around this same period and a solution emerged at that contested monument that was ultimately to provide a strategy to the tourist 'problem' at Newgrange. Stonehenge had an aging visitors' centre as the 1990s dawned and talk of building a new one led to the consideration of a whole new approach to the visitor experience. It was planned that the reception centre for Stonehenge would be placed a mile from the monument and visitors would process along the sacred avenues down to the henge itself, thereby recreating a more authentic experience and at the same time spreading out the numbers amongst the dozens of other significant prehistoric monuments in the immediate vicinity of Stonehenge. This was to be accompanied by the diversion (or tunnelling) of the major road that passes by the site to this day. This was a great idea, but during the Thatcher (and subsequent) years the concept of a self-financing centre took hold, in preference to the concept of investing public monies for the betterment of society.

It is fortunate that Ireland, while always a conservative country, adopted no such doctrinaire approach to public spending. In 1993, at the same time that Newgrange and the entire Bend of the Boyne were listed by UNESCO as a World Heritage Site, the decision was made to build a new visitors' centre on the southern bank of the River Boyne. This award-winning building is massive, especially when compared to previous guide huts, but it is built in such a way that it is almost invisible and near impossible to pick out from Newgrange itself. The Brú na Bóinne Visitor Centre is in a magnificent site, offering the public panoramic views of the Boyne Valley. It has been applauded by the architectural profession as a serious attempt to balance the integrity of important monuments in the landscape and the pressure to provide tourist access to them. There is a feeling of real tranquillity while walking downhill from the car-park along the pergola, beautifully planted with woodbine and many varieties of indigenous trees. This walk allows visitors to wind down after their journey. The walk leads to the upper level of the building where the visitor is gradually guided into the exhibition area and then downstairs to the lower level and ultimately across an elegant cantilever bridge. A series of crooked paths leads to a bus shelter. The geometric plan and prevalent imagery in the detailing of the building brings the visitor on an almost surreal journey into prehistory, with constant reminders of Neolithic culture.

The centre can accommodate four hundred visitors at any one time, and usually does so in the summer months, yet the atmosphere is always relaxed and friendly. There is plenty to see as one waits for the time of their tour. There is a permanent exhibit dealing with the Neolithic as well as temporary exhibits from local artists and craftspeople, and there is a very good restaurant. Although the building was ultimately designed to ease overcrowding, you never get the feeling that you are the harried victim of a 'dispersal strategy' or that you are being 'sustainably managed'. The essential fact is that access to the chamber at Newgrange is possible for about 250,000 visitors every year, with every aspect of the Visitor Centre enhancing that experience. This is largely to the credit of Visitor Services manager for the area, Clare Tuffy, and her staff. As this book is written, she has been in charge of Newgrange for twenty-five years, having taken over directly from Michael Smyth.

The construction of the Visitor Centre has heralded positive changes to the valley. It provides a place of employment for a rural community that was formerly relatively isolated. Local schools have found it a wonderful asset and Clare Tuffy, a former teacher herself, involves school children in many of the

CON BROGAN / DofEH&LG

Fig. 69   Brú na Bóinne Visitor Centre, near the village of Donore in County Meath, acts as a gateway to the World Heritage Site.

centre's activities. The most important event occurs early every December when the names of the lucky winners wishing to witness the winter solstice are picked out by the pupils. The population of the area is pretty small (probably fewer people live in the Bend of the Boyne than during Neolithic times) and the bridge has provided a link for a youth football team made up of members from both sides of the river. Some residents on the north side of the river use the bridge to reach buses serving Donore and Drogheda or just as a place to meet friends and have a cup of coffee. The only downside of the project has been the eclipsing of Slane as the 'gateway' to the Boyne and the small scale tourist industry that had developed on the north side of the river. However, the Celtic Tiger (still roaring away at the time of writing in 2008) has focused most minds on the profits to be made from land sales and housing. Tourism is not nearly so significant economically to the area, which is now essentially part of the greater Dublin hinterland. The new motorway and an excellent train service from Drogheda have copper-fastened this connection.

Neither is the visitor's engagement with the greater Bend of the Boyne area all that it could possibly be. One of the authors of this study has written a book about the region in which the rich heritage of Newgrange and its environs has been described. It has always been our hope that the shuttle bus service would be extended to include hop-on and hop-off points where enthusiasts can visit the wide range of sites in the valley. It is our desire that rights of way will be secured to all points of archaeological and historical interest in the area, enabling visitors to see at first hand why it was the entire region, and not just Newgrange, that was granted World Heritage Site status. Much of this book was written while we visited the Carnac region in Brittany. Rights of way to literally hundreds of sites have been secured, each site features an explanatory plaque, many of the sites have car parks, others are incorporated in exquisitely sign-posted walks, a half-dozen or so have small museums and visitor centres. Something like this needs to be achieved within the Bend of the Boyne. It is also our hope that UNESCO status will provide the impetus for research into the region with funding made available to students and professionals and with a research centre established in which this work could be based. At the time of writing these ambitions have run into the sand but we still hope that they may yet be revived.

While the guides at Newgrange are invariably excellent, their presentations at the passage tomb mainly concern the tomb itself and there is little time to properly contextualise the site. The exhibition in the Visitor Centre makes up for this. It explains, in a very attractive manner, life during the Neolithic period in general and specifically the rich archaeology of the Boyne Valley. It commences with an introduction to the Western European megalithic tomb-building tradition during the Neolithic period. There are then excellent models of the Bend of the Boyne and others that illustrate phases of development at Newgrange. Timelines helpfully orientate the visitor to this distant period of human history. Finds and life-size models bring to life what the everyday world must have been like for Neolithic people: housing, food, clothing; the work in the home, in the fields and on the river. Accompanying these reconstructions, exhibits explain the science behind our understanding of the past; the analysis of bones (and plenty of them, always an item of interest to visitors), radio-carbon dating, pollen analysis and excavation techniques. There is an exhibit on the methods of tomb-building and an audiovisual presentation that explains the astronomy behind the solstice phenomenon at Newgrange. The last room of the exhibition invites the visitor to contemplate the wonders and mystery of passage tomb art. There is, instead of a suggestion box, a place where people can express their own ideas about what the art on the tombs means. This is a refreshing acknowledgement that everyone's opinions about the past are of value and that no one has an absolute monopoly on its 'correct' interpretation.

A great sense of anticipation develops while one waits for the tour of Newgrange itself. Most of us hurry too quickly through the exhibits and leave too early for the bus. When the time of their tour nears, visitors cross the Boyne by a small suspension bridge and are then taken up to Newgrange by bus. The brief walk brings home to us the richness of the valley. Cattle graze the banks. Swans circle in the swirling river. Fish literally jump from the water, making concentric rings of the surface. When the bus from the Visitor Centre reaches the top of McDonnell's lane and turns west along the road at the crest of the ridge, the passage tomb can at last be seen. It is the first glimpse the visitor gets of Newgrange ...

CHAPTER TEN

TRAVEL

Newgrange is more accessible today than it has ever been, thanks to the M1 motorway. To reach the Visitor Centre, take the Donore exit west, the second exit after the toll booth if travelling from Dublin. You still have to pay the toll when exiting if travelling from the north. This is the first exit after the Boyne cable bridge. Brú na Bóinne Visitor Centre is well signposted two kilometres west of the village of Donore. There is parking for two hundred cars at the Centre. The site can be reached from the N2 (the Dublin/Derry road) by turning east at the signposted turnoff two kilometres south of Slane village. This is the most attractive approach to the Centre. From Drogheda you reach Donore by taking the turn opposite McDonalds (there is no better way to describe it) and continuing past the bus station. The Visitor Centre, and therefore Newgrange, can also be accessed by public transport. A half-hourly service to and from Drogheda links this historic medieval town with Dublin to the south and Dundalk to the north. A regular service connects Brú na Bóinne Visitor Centre with the bus station at Drogheda. For those preferring the train, a regular and speedy service links Dublin and Dundalk. Leave Drogheda station and head downhill for a one kilometre walk into the town and then along the river to the bus station. Remember, you cannot access either Newgrange or Knowth from the north side of the river. You must go to the Visitor Centre first.

Most visitors to Newgrange come from Dublin for part of the day only. Newgrange is included in tours organised from the centre of the city, including that organised by Bus Éireann which has left from the main bus station (Bus Áras) since the 1950s. Other companies also include Newgrange in their itineraries.

Those enthusiasts who wish to see both tombs open to the public as well as the many other sites of interest in the Bend of the Boyne might like to stay longer in the area. There are hotels in Drogheda and Slane, hostels in Drogheda, Slane and one beside the Visitor Centre itself. There are many bed-and-breakfast establishments in the area.

As of the time of writing, the Visitor Centre is open all year round, seven days per week, closing only between 24 December and 27 December inclusive. Hours vary throughout the year, with the centre closing at 5 p.m. in winter and at 7 p.m. in summer. The last shuttle bus to the monuments leaves the centre 1 hour and 45 minutes before the centre closes. The number of places available at Newgrange in high season is limited to just over six hundred. On the busiest days during the summer, all the tour places to Newgrange will have sold out by about lunch time. After that there may still

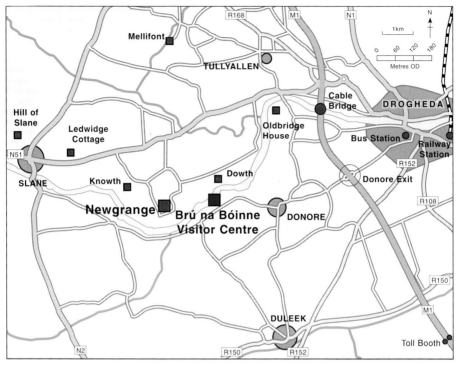

Fig. 70 Location map of Newgrange and environs. Access to the tomb is only possible via the Brú na Bóinne Visitor Centre on the south side of the river.

be availability on visits to Knowth or else to visit the exhibition only. Adult ticket prices for Newgrange (in 2008) were €5.80, with concessions for students and seniors. Tours to Knowth are also available from the Visitor Centre between Easter and the end of October. Reservations are possible for groups by contacting the Visitor Centre by telephone (+353-41-9880300), by fax (+353-41-9823071) but not for individuals. The official website for the Brú na Bóinne Visitor Centre is accessed through www.heritageireland.ie and brunaboinne@opw.ie is the Centre's e-mail address. Even if Newgrange is booked out, the Centre is still worth a visit for its marvellous exhibition, art and craft displays and its restaurant.

Go neirí an bóthar leat.

CHAPTER ELEVEN

SOURCES

This book is our personal synthesis of the archaeology and history of Newgrange and of necessity it is based on the primary investigations of other writers. The most important text and the one kept closest to us during the preparation of this book was M.J. O'Kelly, *Newgrange: archaeology, art and legend* (2nd ed., London: Thames and Hudson, 1994). 'The Wall' and 'The Passage' are almost entirely based on our analysis of O'Kelly's monograph and his personal papers relating to Newgrange.

Chapter 1 – 'The Wall' – incorporates the recent debate over the original appearance of Newgrange: Palle Eriksen, 'Newgrange *og den hvide mur* [Newgrange and the white wall]' in *KUHL*, 2004, pp 45–77; Gabriel Cooney, 'Newgrange – a view from the platform' in *Antiquity*, lxx (2006), pp 697–708; and Chris Scarre, 'Consolidation, reconstruction and the interpretation of megalithic monuments' in R. Cruz and L. Oosterbeek (eds), *ARKEOS – Perspectives em diálogo*, xvi (2006), pp 13–43.

The origins of the stones at Newgrange have been analysed in: G. Frank Mitchell, 'Notes on some non-local cobbles at the entrance to the passage-graves at Newgrange and Knowth, County Meath' in *Journal of the Royal Society of Antiquaries of Ireland*, cxxii (1992), pp 128–45; Adrian Phillips, Mary Corcoran and George Eogan, *Identification of the source area for megaliths used in the construction of the Neolithic passage graves of the Boyne Valley, County Meath* (unpublished report for The Heritage Council, Ireland, 2002); I.G. Meighan, D.D.A. Simpson, B.N. Hartwell, A.E. Fallick, P.S. Kennan, 'Sourcing the quartz at Newgrange, Brú na Bóinne, Ireland' in G. Burenhult and S. Westergaard (eds), *Stones and bones: formal disposal of the dead in Atlantic Europe during the Mesolithic–Neolithic interface 6000–3000 BC. Archaeological conference in honour of the late Michael J. O'Kelly* (BAR International Series 1201, Oxford: British Archaeological Reports, 2003), pp 247–51.

For Chapters 2 and 3 – 'The Entrance' and 'The Passage' – the key primary source for the art at Newgrange is the work of Claire O'Kelly, especially her *Illustrated guide to Newgrange and the other Boyne monuments* (3rd ed., Cork: Claire O'Kelly, 1978); 'Corpus of Newgrange art' in M.J. O'Kelly *Newgrange*, part iv, pp 146-85 and 'Passage-grave art in the Boyne Valley' in *Proceedings of the Prehistoric Society*, xxxix, pp 354-82. Other works essential to understanding passage tomb art are: Elizabeth Shee Twohig, *The Megalithic Art of Western Europe* (Oxford: Clarendon Press, 1981) and '"Megalithic art" in a settlement context: Skara Brae and related sites in the Orkney Islands' in *Brigantium*, x (1997), pp 377–89; Muiris O'Sullivan, *Megalithic Art in Ireland*, (Dublin: TownHouse and Country House, 1993), 'Megalithic art in the Boyne

Valley' in *Brú na Bóinne*; supplement to *Archaeology Ireland*, xi (1997), pp 36–7, and 'The art of the passage tomb at Knockroe, County Kilkenny' in *Journal of the Royal Society of Antiquaries of Ireland*, cxvii (1987), pp 84–95. The possibility that megalithic art has its origins in hallucinations is examined in three articles by Jeremy Dronfield in 'Migraine, light and hallucinogens: the neurocognitive basis of Irish megalithic art' in *Oxford Journal of Archaeology*, xiv (1995), pp 261–75; 'Subjective vision and the source of Irish megalithic art' in *Antiquity*, lxix (1995), pp 539–49 and 'Entering alternative realities: cognition, art and architecture in Irish passage-tombs' in *Cambridge Archaeological Journal*, vi (1996), pp 37–72. The acoustic properties of passage tombs are examined in Paul Devereux and Robert G. Jahn, 'Preliminary investigations and cognitive considerations of the acoustical resonances of selected archaeological sites' in *Antiquity*, lxx (1996), pp 665–6 and in Aaron Watson and David Keating, 'Architecture and sound: an acoustic analysis of megalithic monuments in prehistoric Britain' in *Antiquity*, lxxiii (1999), pp 325–36. The use of colour by megalithic tomb-builders is examined in Frances Lynch, 'Colour in prehistoric architecture' in Alex Gibson and Derek Simpson (eds), *Prehistoric ritual and religion: essays in honour of Aubrey Burl* (Gloucestershire: Sutton, 1998), pp 62–7. George Eogan, *Knowth and the passage-tombs of Ireland* (London: Thames and Hudson, 1986) and Michael Herity, *Irish passage graves: Neolithic tomb-builders in Ireland and Britain 2500 B.C.* (Dublin: Irish University Press, 1974) were also useful.

Chapter 4 – 'Solstice' – is based on O'Kelly's publications and detailed drawings preserved in the O'Kelly Archive. Further insights are provided in two conference papers by Frank Prendergast: 'In the eye of the beholder: symbolism and meaning in Irish Passage tomb alignment and height', paper submitted to UISPP, XV, 2006, Symposium C52, Cognitive archaeology as symbiotic archaeology; and 'Visual signatures in the Irish Neolithic landscape: a wider perspective on the Irish passage tombs', paper submitted to lights and shadows in cultural astronomy conference, Italy 2006.

Knowth by Eogan and *Irish passage graves* by Herity were indispensable in preparing chapter 5 – 'Ritual' – as was M.J. O'Kelly, Frances Lynch and Claire O'Kelly, 'Three passage graves at Newgrange, County Meath' in *Proceedings of the Royal Irish Academy*, C, lxxviii (1978), pp 249–352.

Chapter 6 – 'Life' – examines Neolithic life and environment in the Boyne Valley. It is drawn from the results of the excavations at Newgrange, mainly from O'Kelly's monograph but see also Seán P. Ó Ríordáin and Marcus P. Ó hEochaidhe, 'Trial excavations at Newgrange' in *Journal of the Royal Society of Antiquaries of Ireland*, lxxxvi (1956), pp 52–61. This chapter owes a great deal to works by Gabriel Cooney: 'Irish Neolithic landscapes and land use systems: the implications of field systems' in *Rural History*, ii (1991), pp 123–39; *Landscapes of Neolithic Ireland* (London: Routledge, 2000); Cooney and Eoin Grogan, *Irish prehistory: a social perspective* (Dublin: Wordwell, 1994). See also Geraldine Stout, *Newgrange and the Bend of the Boyne* (Cork: Cork University Press, 2002). None of this work would have been possible without the knowledge and encouragement of the Boyne Valley's greatest scholar, Frank Mitchell. For his work on environmental aspects of Newgrange in prehistory, see 'Did the tide once flow as far as Newgrange?' in *Living Heritage*, xii (1995), p. 34 and 'The geology of the Bend of the Boyne' in *Brú na Bóinne*, supplement to *Archaeology Ireland,* xi (1997), pp 5–6.

Chapter 7 – 'Roots' – examines the origins of the Neolithic in the Bend of the Boyne. It has made use of publications available in the English language dealing with French and Spanish megaliths: Charles-Tanguy Le Roux, 'The art of Gavrinis presented in its Armorican context and in comparison with Ireland' in *Journal of the Royal Society of Antiquaries of Ireland*, cxxii (1992), pp 79–108; Charles-Tanguy Le Roux, 'New excavations at Gavrinis' in *Antiquity*, lix (1985), pp 183–7; Jacques Briard, *The megaliths of Brittany* (Locon, France: Éditions Gisserot, 1997); Jean L'Helgoac'h, *Locmariaquer* (French language edition, Locon, France: Éditions Gisserot, 2004); Pierre-Roland Giot, *Prehistory in Brittany: menhirs and dolmens* (Chateaulin, France: Éditions D'Art, 2004); Chris Scarre, Luc LaPorte and Roger Joussaume, 'Long mounds and megalithic origins in Western France: recent excavations at Prissé-la-Charrière' in *Proceedings of the Prehistoric Society*, lxix (2003), pp 235–51. The excavation and reconstruction of the important passage tomb in Alcalar, southern Portugal is presented in Elana Morán and Rui Parreira (eds), *Alcalar 7: estudo e reabiltação de um moumento megalítico* (Lisboa: Instituto Português do Património Arquitectónico, 2004). Valuable insights are also available in: George Eogan, 'Megalithic art and society' in *Proceedings of the Prehistoric Society*, lxv (1999), pp 415–46; George Eogan, 'Irish megalithic tombs and Iberia: comparisons and contrasts' in Walter de Gruyer, *Problee der megalithgruberforschung* (Madrider Forschungen, Band 16. Berlin), pp 113–37; J.-P. Mohen, *The world of megaliths* (New York: Facts on File, 1990). Welsh links are examined in Frances Lynch, 'Barclodiad y Gawres' in *Archaeologia Cambrensis,* cxvii (1967), pp 1–22. We availed of recent works on megalithic chronologies in Europe: Chris Scarre, Pablo Arias, Goran Burenhult, Miguel Fano, Luiz Oosterbeek, Rick Schulting, Alison Sheridan and Alasdair Whittle, 'Megalithic Chronologies' in Burenhult and Westergaard (eds), *Stones and bones,* pp 65–94; and Alison Sheridan, 'Ireland's earliest 'passsage' tombs: a French connection?' in Burenhult and Westergaard (eds), *Stones and bones,* pp 9–25. Eoin Grogan's 'Appendix: radiocarbon dates from Brugh na Boinne' in George Eogan, 'Prehistoric and early historic culture change at Brugh na Boinne' in *Proceedings of the Royal Irish Academy*, C, xci (1991), pp 105–32. Pages 126–7 provide a wonderfully straightforward compendium of all the radiocarbon dates from the Bend of the Boyne.

As was noted in Chapter 8 – 'The Great Stone Circle' – the key to understanding the Bronze Age at Newgrange began with the discoveries by David Sweetman, 'A Late Neolithic/Early Bronze Age pit circle at Newgrange, County Meath' in *Proceedings of the Royal Irish Academy*, C, lxxxv (1985), pp 195–221 and 'Excavations of a Late Neolithic/Early Bronze Age site at Newgrange, County Meath' in *Proceedings of the Royal Irish Academy*, C, lxxvii (1987), pp 283–98. A clear overview of the Beaker activity is provided in Charles Mount, 'Aspects of ritual deposition in the Late Neolithic and Beaker periods at Newgrange, County Meath' in *Proceedings of the Prehistoric Society*, lx (1994), pp 433–43. Richard Bradley, 'Stone circles and passage graves – a contested relationship' in Alex Gibson and Derek Simpson (eds), *Prehistoric ritual and religion: essays in honour of Aubrey Burl* (Gloucestershire: Sutton, 1998), pp 2–13 provides an argument against the accepted Bronze Age chronology at Newgrange. The excavation report, Claire O'Kelly (ed.), *Newgrange, Co. Meath, Ireland: the Late Neolithic/Beaker Period settlement* (Oxford: BAR International Series 190, 1983) should be read in the light of the later discoveries. This excavation report features M.J. O'Kelly, 'The excavation', pp 1–57; Rose M. Cleary, 'The ceramic assemblage' pp 58–117; and Daragh Lehane, 'The flint work', pp 118–67. See also M.J. O'Kelly and C. Shell, 'Some objects and a bronze axe from Newgrange, county Meath' in M. Ryan (ed.), *Origins of metallurgy in Atlantic Europe* (Dublin: Stationery Office, 1979), pp 127–44. The animal bones uncovered at Newgrange were the subject of Louise Hilgonda van Wijngaarden–Bakker's pioneering doctoral research published as: 'The animal bones from the Beaker settlement at Newgrange, County Meath: first report' *in Proceedings of the Royal Irish Academy*, C, lxxiv (1974), pp 313–83; *An archaeological study of the Beaker settlement at Newgrange, Ireland* (Amsterdam: Wijngaarden–Bakker, 1980); 'The animal remains from the Beaker settlement at Newgrange, County Meath: final report' in *Proceedings of the Royal Irish Academy*, C, lxxxvi (1986), pp 2–111. For a wider perspective on Early Bronze Age Newgrange, see Geraldine Stout, 'Embanked enclosures of the Boyne region' in *Proceedings of the Royal Irish Academy*, xci (1991), C, pp 245–84. Analysis of the astronomic alignments of the Great Stone Circle are discussed in Frank Prendergast, 'New data on Newgrange' in *Technology Ireland*, xxii (1991), pp 22–5 and 'Shadow-casting phenomena at Newgrange' in *Survey Ireland*, ix (1991), pp 9–18. A Scottish parallel for shadow-casting is discussed in David Trevarthen, 'Illuminating the monuments: observation and speculation on the structure and function of the cairns at Balnuaran of Clava' in *Cambridge Archaeological Journal*, x (2000), pp 295–315. Clive Ruggles, *Astronomy in prehistoric Britain and Ireland* (New Haven and London: Yale University Press, 1999) provides the most level-headed analysis of prehistoric alignments. Anthony Murphy and Richard Moore, *Island of the setting sun: in search of Ireland's ancient astronomers* (Dublin: The Liffey Press, 2006) has many original and valuable ideas about Newgrange and early astronomy.

Chapter 9 – 'Ruins' – called on a wide range of sources. Roman finds from Newgrange are clearly analysed in R.A.G. Carson and Claire O'Kelly, 'A catalogue of the Roman coins from Newgrange, Co. Meath and notes on the coins and related finds' in *Proceedings of the Royal Irish Academy*, C, lxxvii (1977), pp 35-55. See also J.D. Bateson, 'Roman material from Ireland: a re–consideration' in *Proceedings of the Royal Irish Academy*, C, lxxiii (1973), pp 21–97. The Early Christian sources for the site are detailed in Geraldine

Stout's *Newgrange*, Elizabeth Hickey provides a lively retelling of the early legends in *I send my love along the Boyne* (Dublin: Allen Figgis, 1966, republished Drogheda, Ireland: Áine Ní Chairbre, 2000). Medieval activity at Newgrange is described in M.J. O'Kelly, 'Plough pebbles from the Boyne Valley' in C. Ó Danachair (ed.), *Folk and farm: essays in honour of A.T. Lucas* (Dublin: Royal Society of Antiquaries of Ireland, 1976), pp 165–75. This paper on plough pebbles clearly shows the breadth of Professor O'Kelly's interests and discoveries.

The antiquarian history of Newgrange is addressed most thoroughly in O'Kelly's *Newgrange* and Herity's *Irish passage tombs*, but for additional material see Michael Herity, 'From Lhuyd to Coffey: new information from unpublished descriptions of the Boyne valley tombs' in *Studia Hibernica*, vii (1967), pp 127–45 and Anthony Candon, 'An early nineteenth-century description of Newgrange, County Meath' in *Journal of the Royal Society of Antiquaries*, cxiv (1984), pp 24–7. The original antiquarian material is always worth reading, especially the unsurpassed William Wilde, *The Beauties of the Boyne and Blackwater* (Dublin: James McGlashan, 1849). See also T. Pownall, 'A description of the sepulchral monument at Newgrange, near Drogheda, in the county of Meath, in Ireland' in *Archaeologia*, ii (1773), pp 236–75 and T. Molyneaux, 'A discourse concerning the Danish mounts, forts and towers in Ireland' in G. Boate (ed.), *A natural history of Ireland* (London: Chetham Society, 1725).

The quotation about the mysteries of Newgrange from Nano Reid comes from a ground-breaking book about Drogheda's foremost artist. Her work is now beginning to be appreciated and highly valued as her biography deserves to be: Declan Mallon, *Nano Reid 1900–1981* (Drogheda: Declan Mallon, 1994). For Newgrange and spirituality see Hugh Gash and Mary Shine Thompson, 'Constructivism and Celtic spirituality: beginning a discussion', paper read to the International Symposium on Culture of Peace, Baden Baden, Germany, 2002. The following publications provide a selection of 'New Age' interpretations of Newgrange. This gives a good indication that the excavations have not closed down debate about the site's purpose. We confess to not having read every word of these books: Martin Brennan, *The Boyne Valley vision* (Mountrath, Ireland: The Dolmen Press, 1980); *The stars and the stones: ancient art and astronomy in Ireland* (London: Thames and Hudson, 1983); *The stones of time: calendars, sundials and stone chambers of ancient Ireland* (Rochester, VT: Inner traditions, Bear and Company, 1994). Brennan has also 'discovered' the secrets to Maya hieroglyphics in *The hidden Maya* (Rochester, VT: Inner traditions, Bear and Company, 1998). See also R. Iyer and N. Iyer, *The descent of Gods: comprising the mystical writings of G.W. Russell 'A.E.'* (Gerrards Cross, Buckinghamshire: Dufour Editions, 1989); Michael Poynder, *Pi in the sky: a revelation of the wisdom tradition* (London: Rider, 1992); J. Westwood (ed.), *Sacred Journeys: paths for the new pilgrim* (London: Gaia Books, 1997); D.L. Cyr, *Cascading comets: the key to ancient mysteries* (Santa Barbara, California: Stonehenge Viewpoint, 1998); D.

Sullivan, *Ley Lines: a comprehensive guide to alignments* (London: Piatkus Books, 2000); Chris O'Callaghan, *Newgrange, temple to life: a re-interpretation* (Cork: Mercier Press, 2004).

The section on tourism profited from the following publications: Liam Mac Uistin, *Exploring Newgrange* (Dublin: O'Brien Press, 1999) and Seán P. Ó Ríordáin and Glyn Daniel, *New Grange and the Bend of the Boyne* (London: Thames and Hudson, 1964). See also George Coffey, *New Grange and other incised tumuli in Ireland* (Dublin: Hodges Figgis and Co., 1912, reprinted Poole Dorset: The Dolphin Press, 1977) and Geraldine Stout, *The Bend of the Boyne: an archaeological landscape* (Dubin: TownHouse and Country House, 1997). Travellers' accounts of Newgrange and environs can be found in Chevalier de Latocnaye, (John Stevenson, trans.), *A Frenchman's walk through Ireland, 1796–7* (reprinted Belfast: Blackstaff, 1984); Charlotte Elizabeth [Tonna], *Letters from Ireland 1837* (London: Seely and Burnside, 1838); Johann Georg Kohl, *Travels in Ireland* (London: Bruce and Wyld, 1844); and Michael Myers Shoemaker, *Wanderings in Ireland* (New York and London: Putnam, 1908). The Visitor Centre is discussed in Eugene Keane, 'The visitor centre: gateway to Brú na Bóinne' in *Brú na Bóinne*; supplement to *Archaeology Ireland*, xi (1997), pp 36–7; Anthony O'Neill Architects and Niall McCullough, 'Brú na Bóinne Visitor Centre, Donore, Co. Meath' in *Irish Architect: the Journal of the Royal Institute of the Architects of Ireland*, cxxix (1997), pp 27–35; Maggie Ronayne, 'The political economy of landscape: conflict and value in a prehistoric landscape in the Republic of Ireland – ways of telling' in Barbara Bender and Margot Winer (eds), *Contested landscapes: movement, exile and place* (Oxford: Berg, 2001), pp 149–64.

INDEX

(Page numbers in italics refer to illustrations and captions)